THE FINAL BET

A Memoir of Love and Legacy

Amos Hadad

AMI Publishing CO.
Fort Lauderdale, FL

Published by **AMI Publishing CO.**
Fort Lauderdale, FL

ISBN (print): 979-8-90321-044-2
ISBN (ebook): 979-8-2956-9264-2
ISBN (audiobook):
First edition

Editorial & Design Credits
Editorial direction / Project editor: **Amos Hadad**
Copyediting & proofreading: **Amos Hadad** (final review)
Cover design: [Name or **"AMI Publishing CO."**]
Interior design & typesetting: **AMI Publishing CO.**
Author photo: **[Name]**
Production management: **AMI Publishing CO.**

This is a work of nonfiction. Some names and identifying details may have been changed to protect privacy. Certain scenes and conversations are reconstructed from the author's best recollection, notes, and contemporaneous records.

Nothing in this book constitutes legal, tax, medical, or financial advice. Readers should consult qualified professionals for guidance specific to their circumstances.

Library of Congress Control Number: [to be requested] (optional)
Trademarks are the property of their respective owners.
Printed in the United States of America
10 9 8 7 6 5 4 3 2 1

Dedications:

For my father
this book is in your honor and memory.

For my mother
the backbone and quiet strength; without you, carrying
through would have been a different kind of challenge.

For my wife
my anchor and counterpart.

For my children
remember who your grandfather was.
Let this be a guiding light, not just a story.

For my brothers and sisters
who shared the blows and the blessings,
the challenges and the celebrations,
the good times and the great.

**And for every entrepreneur who carries the roar of
a lion**
build with courage and protect what you build.

Table of Contents

Part I

Part II

Part I

Prologue:
The Final Bet

In gambling lore, the final bet isn't placed at the table.

It's made in silence, when no one's watching, and there's no time left to hedge.

The real stakes aren't in chips. They're in consequences.

This book began as a tribute, but it became something more honest, a reckoning.

At first, I thought I was writing only to preserve the stories, to capture the legacy of a man who built everything from nothing, who fed seven mouths on instinct, who lived like a lion and moved like a myth. But as the memories poured in, so did something deeper: a truth that demanded to be told.

Hanavi, my father, didn't believe in blueprints. He believed in motion.

When others planned, he pivoted.

When others hesitated, he acted.

He never asked permission, not from partners, not from fate.

He played the hand he was dealt like it was rigged in his favor.

And for a while, it was.

He made strangers feel like royalty. He could walk into a room and shift its gravity. He could charm anyone, turn nothing into something, and create opportunities out of thin air. He didn't just chase opportunity, he was opportunity.

But beneath the bravado was a man carrying the weight of a broken childhood, the silence of abandonment, and a vow never to feel powerless again. His life was built on instinct, not insulation. Momentum was his only strategy.

No insurance.

No will.

No fallback.

No instructions.

Just motion, and memory.

And when the motion stopped, everything else unraveled, his empire, his health, his voice, his body. The house he once ruled fell into decay. The name he had spent decades building became a whisper. And those left behind, his wife, his children, his legacy, were left to sweep up what never had walls to begin with.

He wasn't a planner. He was a player.

He gambled with his moves, not always in casinos, though he was no stranger to the felt, but in life itself: business deals, real estate, relationships, reputation. Every day was a bet. Every hand, a wager.

And for a time, that gamble gave us life.

But gamblers always face the final bet.

I didn't grow up with the language of protection.

We had hustle, motion, survival. But we didn't have a roadmap. No one sat us down to explain wills, trusts, tax shelters, or life insurance. No one taught us what happens when a provider can no longer provide. We knew how to stretch a dollar, how to keep moving, how to survive, but not how to preserve.

The wealthy live differently. They don't just build wealth; they build systems to sustain it. Their children grow up knowing what a trust is, how insurance works, how to compound wealth instead of just chasing it. They understand that

Legacy isn't what you leave when you die, it's what you structure while you live.

My father never learned that. Neither did I, not until it was too late to learn from him.

So, this book isn't only his story. It's mine, too.

I'm 45 as I write these words. Two marriages. Three children. No fortune yet, just stories and scars. I live surrounded by love, but love alone doesn't pay bills, doesn't build futures, doesn't protect legacies. I've had to learn the hard way that love without structure becomes struggle.

Youth is the strongest asset, and we waste it chasing everything but stability.

Today's generation wants freedom fast, TikTok riches, Instagram lifestyles, retire-by-thirty schemes. I see it, because I chased the same illusions.

But

Motion without planning is just noise.

And when the music stops, if you don't have structure... you're not a visionary. You're a cautionary tale.

Walt Disney borrowed against his life insurance to build Disneyland.

J.C. Penney used his to pay employees during the Great Depression.

Ray Kroc used his to expand McDonald's.

Doris Christopher used one to build Pampered Chef, and sold it to Warren Buffett.

These weren't accidents.

They were structured plays.

When I woke up to this truth, the first thing I did was buy a term policy. Not much. Not glamorous. Just what I could afford. But it was a start, a safety net so my family wouldn't be left pawning heirlooms, if any remained, to survive.

That's when I realized something:

The bet isn't whether you win or lose.

The bet is whether you're protected first.

Because if you're covered, structured, stable, then you can take risks. You can chase vision. You can dream and build. You can sit at the table and play the hand.

But if you gamble.

*Without protection, without foundation...
you're not building legacy, you're
borrowing time.*

This story is about my father. But it's also about every man who's lived loud, hustled hard, and left nothing but motion behind. It's about what happens when instinct replaces planning, when pride replaces protection, and when silence leaves the people you love with questions instead of answers.

Everyone who knew him has their own version of him. This is mine, the son's view from the passenger seat, from the locked office doors, from the poker chips stacked like prayers.

And if there's one lesson that echoes across every chapter, it's this:

You can't outrun planning.

You can't bet on forever.

And the final wager isn't made at the table. It's made in the choices we avoid.

Eventually, even lions run out of roars.

And when the music fades, all that's left are the echoes.

This book is my father's story.

But maybe, if you let it, it can become yours too.

Because.

The final bet we all face is thinking we still have time.

Chapter 1:
The Gambler's Mind

Hanavi never followed a script. His life moved fast, instinct-driven, emotionally armored, and powered by motion. Born in 1958 in Israel, one of eight siblings, he came from a family of migrants who had survived displacement, disillusionment, and silence.

His parents were Jewish immigrants from Tunisia, part of a large wave of North African Jews who fled persecution, anti-Semitic violence, and collapsing colonial rule following World War II. As Arab nationalism surged through the Maghreb, Jewish communities in places like Tunisia, Algeria, and Morocco were pushed out, many migrating to Israel during the 1950s mass aliyah that reshaped the Jewish diaspora. Hanavi's family, like thousands of others, arrived with little more than identity, language, and stubborn pride.

His father, a butcher by trade, was quiet, stern, and emotionally restrained. His mother, employed in a classified military role, was often gone. Love in their household was conditional. Comfort was earned. Control was survival.

At 18, Hanavi was drafted into the Israeli military, where he served as a military police officer and aviation mechanic. The army gave him order, but never softened his rough edges. He played soccer with a vengeance, screamed over goals while spitting sunflower seeds, and carried an energy that never sat still.

During his service, Hanavi rode a moped to get around the base. When money was tight, and it often was, he "borrowed" fuel from base reserves. One day, he was caught. The punishment was simple but sharp: detainment. Even for small offenses, military justice was swift.

Being locked up, even briefly, left a scar. Hanavi never forgot the silence, the loss of agency. That moment would define him for decades. He vowed never again to give anyone power over his freedom. From then on, his life would be built around control, total, unflinching, and personal.

That was when fate began whispering.

On a rare weekend home from base, Hanavi was hanging around the neighborhood when he noticed his sister sitting at a café with some friends. One of them caught his eye, a quiet girl, soft-featured, withdrawn. She was focused on school, preparing for her upcoming military draft, and had no interest in meeting anyone.

But something about her stuck.

Later, he casually asked his sister, "Who is she?" He wasn't concerned whether she was interested or not. That didn't matter. His curiosity had already taken root.

Not long after, they all went to the movies, a common pastime for teenagers. Israeli cinemas at the time mainly showed Turkish or Bollywood dramas, dubbed or subtitled, often filled with sweeping romantic plots and themes of betrayal, loyalty, and destiny. That night's film was one of those Turkish melodramas, full of brooding stares and tragic lovers, the kind of movie where everything changes in one decisive moment.

Midway through, his sister excused herself to use the restroom. Hanavi entered the dark theater and took her seat.

He said nothing. Neither did she.

But that quiet, flickering moment would change both their lives.

The girl was 17. Her military paperwork was nearly complete. But Hanavi had already made his decision. He approached her father, asked for her hand in marriage, and received his blessing.

They married in 1978, he was 20, she was 18.

In the summer of 1979, their first child, a son, was born. And now, Hanavi's hustle wasn't optional, it was essential.

He turned to what he knew: poker, rummy, flipping appliances, buying low and selling fast. He never held still. Everything was negotiable. Every night was a chance to earn. By 1982, after the birth of their daughter, his second child, Hanavi raised enough capital to partner with an army friend and open a VHS rental and electronics shop.

Black-and-white TVs. Radios. Beta tapes. VHS movies. They were early in the game, and profitable.

But it was all motion.

No insulation.

No protection.

No plan.

Hanavi was building a life.

But not yet a legacy.

Chapter 2: The Cost of Winning

By 1985, Hanavi and his wife had three children. Their eldest son was eight, their daughter five, and their youngest, a two-year-old boy, was just learning to speak in full sentences. They lived modestly in Israel, surrounded by nearby family but crowded by financial pressure. The apartment was loud, small, and pulsing with unspoken limitations.

Hanavi felt the walls tightening around him. His instinct, a force that had guided him through every pivot and hustle, told him to move. So he did.

Without waiting for consensus, he boarded a plane to America alone. It was the mid-1980s. That final night before the flight, a few close friends and confidants came by, not just any acquaintances, but the ones he trusted most. The men he shared soccer matches with, who understood not just his strategies but his fire. They were more than friends. They were co-dreamers, partners in sweat, risk, and motion. The apartment buzzed with subdued conversation: "early morning," "documents," "luggage," "America."

Hanavi's eldest son overheard something about a plane.

"I want to go on a plane," he said aloud.

One of the men turned, smiled faintly, and said, "Well… we're about to."

They arrived in Philadelphia in 1988, three children in tow and a fourth still in the womb. Their first stop was a worn-down motel off Roosevelt Boulevard in Northeast Philadelphia, a roadside inn with a flickering sign, a vending machine in the lobby, and a single room where suitcases doubled as dressers. It was tight, but it was something. The whole experience was something new.

The next morning brought their first American breakfast.

Eggs were familiar, but not like this. What arrived on the plates was an "omelette", thick, fluffy, stuffed with vegetables and melted cheese. Alongside it, crispy golden potatoes. Home fries, the waitress had called them. The children stared. The parents chewed slowly, quietly. It was simple food, but it tasted like a new beginning.

Once the family scraped together enough income, they left the motel and moved into a narrow brick rowhome just a few blocks away. It was a townhouse-style unit, three bedrooms, two baths, stacked wall-to-wall with identical homes. There was no backyard, just a small concrete slab behind a rusting gate. But inside, it was clean, practical, and enough room to get by in comfort. The floor creaked. The kids shared rooms. But it was theirs. And for the first time since leaving Israel, it felt like solid ground.

Their next-door neighbor was a woman raising her son on her own. Over time, the family learned she was the wife, perhaps estranged, of Joe Frazier, the former heavyweight champion of the world. For those unfamiliar, Joe Frazier wasn't just any boxer, he was the man who defeated Muhammad Ali in the legendary 1971 Fight of the Century, and went twelve brutal rounds in the punishing Thrilla in Manila. A southpaw with a hook like thunder and a legacy etched in sweat and steel.

His son was just a year or two older than Hanavi's eldest, and sometimes the kids played on the stoop or peeked at each other across the porch steps. Every so often, Joe himself would visit.

He never stayed long, but when he pulled up, the entire block seemed to hold its breath. People peered through blinds. Kids paused mid-play. Adults stood a little straighter. He always greeted the neighbors warmly, his gravelly voice and heavy hands giving off a presence you didn't just notice, you felt it. On rare occasions, he'd pose for photos, offer a nod, maybe a quick story. And for a family fresh off the plane from Israel, it felt surreal.

There, in the middle of Northeast Philly, in a quiet rowhome, they lived beside a living legend. And for first-timers trying to grasp what "America" really was, Joe Frazier's unannounced visits made the myth feel real, the kind of awe you don't just witness, you carry.

Hanavi worked endlessly.

By day, he fixed cars in a local garage. By night, he drove a cab through neighborhoods he barely recognized. English was still a daily hurdle, but he got by on grit and instinct. Sleep came in fragments. Bills came in full.

And still, when guests visited from Israel, Hanavi played the part. But it was his wife who laid out the food, arranged the plates, and catered not only to his needs but to theirs as well. She smiled through the fatigue, her hospitality unfolding as quietly as his ambition roared. No one saw the unopened envelopes stacked behind a drawer, except for her, who silently carried the weight.

The cards followed him into this new life.

Poker. Blackjack. The felt became his side hustle, his insurance policy, his way of creating stretch where there was none. Some nights he lost. Others he walked away ahead. But always, the risk was just beneath the surface, calculated, familiar.

Like Dostoevsky's unnamed gambler, Hanavi wasn't just chasing the high of a win, he was seduced by the very act of risking everything. The roulette wheel in Dostoevsky's fiction symbolized the chaos of fate wrapped in illusory control. For Hanavi, the poker table offered no real order, only a momentary stage where instincts roared louder than reason, and losing often masqueraded as living.

When the wins came, he shared them. Outings to his favorite destinations, Atlantic City, especially the Boardwalk, where neon lights buzzed against the ocean breeze and the scent of funnel cakes, salt, and sea clung to every breath. For the kids, the rides, blinking Ferris wheels, gravity-defying swings, the laughter of strangers, felt like magic. For Hanavi, it was the casinos: the Trump Taj Mahal, with its marble floors, gaudy chandeliers, and towers that seemed to scrape the clouds. To a hustler like him, it was paradise wrapped in risk.

It wasn't just about the cards. It was about being somewhere that felt impossible to reach, and knowing he got them there.

These weren't just indulgences.

They were rituals.

They were dreams made briefly real.

The trips would typically start with a dinner, or end with one. A steakhouse. A family meal with tablecloths. The kind of place where you didn't ask the price first. Where the kids ordered what they wanted. Where Hanavi paid with the confidence of a man who made the win mean something. Then it was back on the road, full from more than food.

These moments weren't escapes.

They were offerings.

Proof that all the chaos and hustle had meaning.

But beneath every smile, the numbers waited.

The rent.

The tuition.

The gas.

The groceries.

He wasn't playing to win.

He was playing not to lose.

TRUMP
PLAZA
BALLY'S
Showboat
TAXI

Chapter 3:
The Ante

The snow was still melting off the gutters when Hanavi put the down payment on the house. Northeast Philadelphia. Red brick. Built in 1958, the same year he was born. A corner lot with a patchy front lawn, a narrow driveway, and enough square footage to raise a dynasty.

It wasn't grand. But it was his.

He didn't throw a celebration. He didn't dance in the kitchen or call everyone to come see. He simply stood in the doorway, silent, scanning the walls like a man surveying potential. And then he went to work, not with tools, but with vision.

Hanavi didn't tighten hinges or fix pipes, not yet. He eyed the corners, studied the structure, and began to visualize. He saw what wasn't there yet. Not just a house, but a stronghold. A seed. A place where he could inscribe his name in more than just drywall. He didn't move in, he took ownership.

In his mind, it wasn't just a house. It was the first brick in the foundation of a legacy. A generational compound. A place where sons wouldn't scatter, where siblings could live within walking distance, where laughter and loyalty lived on the same block. No nursing homes. No rented spaces. Just Friday nights under one roof.

For once, the space didn't feel like a rental.

And life, though still heavy, had started to take shape.

By the early fall of 1990, that foundation grew deeper. A daughter was born, their fifth child. Her cry filled the kitchen, her crib overtook the dining room corner, and her presence changed the rhythm of the home. Life was still hard. Money was still tight. And yet, every Friday night, the table was set.

No matter how broke they were, or how tired his wife was, Shabbat was non-negotiable, a sacred pause in a week of chaos. White tablecloth. Candles lit. Wine poured. She prepared the meals, sometimes stretched thinner than they should be, but never short on care. Her fingers moved with ritual. Her eyes carried fatigue, but also pride.

When guests came, and they always came, Hanavi greeted them. But it was his wife who fed them. Cousins visiting from Israel. Siblings. In-laws. Depending on whose side of the family it was, the dynamic shifted, but the door never closed. Hospitality was law. Not performative, but personal.

These rituals weren't just acts of faith.

They weren't rebellion against the home he came from.

They were his controlled version of the home he wanted to see.

Eventually, the Kiddush, the blessing over the wine, was passed to his eldest son. Not with ceremony. Just a glance. A nod. Maybe it was tradition. Maybe it was symbolic. Maybe it was just Hanavi's way of saying, "This part isn't mine anymore." A quiet relief of duty.

Meanwhile, the business was growing.

He had leased a small corner garage in North Philadelphia, nothing flashy, just enough room for a lift and a prayer. The neighborhood was gritty, traffic-heavy, and full of potential. He started alone. Then hired a helper. Then bought his first wreck at auction, patched it up, and sold it to someone who needed wheels.

Word spread fast. But it wasn't just the service.

Hanavi made people feel like they mattered. He offered tools. Jobs. Advice. Old cabbies with bad backs. Young hustlers trying to get started. Some became regulars. Some became loyalists. Some became lifelong friends. And even when the workday ended, the garage stayed alive with talk and motion.

It wasn't just a repair shop.

It was a command post.

Eventually, he began renting out bays to other mechanics, just one at first, then another. The space became a hub, not an empire yet, but the scaffolding of one. A place where ambition smelled like oil and sounded like possibility.

Hanavi would come home late, body sore from the grind. He didn't complain loudly, but the toll showed. Every evening, he'd settle onto the couch, motioning to his wife without a word. She knew the look. She'd kneel quietly, help him pull off his shoes, and rub his feet or legs as he exhaled from the day.

It wasn't affection in words.

It was in ritual.

In knowing. In showing up.

He never needed to ask twice.

And as he lay there, shoulders down, eyes toward the ceiling, the garage still buzzing in his mind, he'd whisper, often to no one in particular:

"Still in the game."

He wasn't rich.

But he was rooted.

And for the first time in years, he wasn't just surviving.

He was building.

Chapter 4:
Raising the Stakes

By the early 1990s, the family's life in Northeast Philadelphia had reached a pivotal rhythm. Hanavi was running both a modest automotive shop and a cab operation, managing dispatches, overseeing car deals, and always keeping one eye on the numbers and the other on momentum. But his mind was never just in the day-to-day. He was always watching for the next bet, something that could change their position permanently.

That next bet started to take shape during a deeply symbolic moment: his eldest son's Bar Mitzvah.

It wasn't just a religious rite, it was a full production. Nearly 200 guests arrived: business associates, childhood friends, old faces from Israel. For the first time since his own wedding, both sides of the family were under the same roof. The house buzzed with energy and pride. Every detail had been curated to reflect one truth: we've made it.

The house, for that weekend, overflowed with joy and purpose. Guests spilled into the kitchen, down the hallway, onto the back patio. It wasn't just a celebration of his son's transition into manhood, it was Hanavi's victory lap. A quiet declaration that momentum was no longer a gamble. It was reality. He had built something real, and for once, it was being seen.

Around this time, Hanavi made one of his most forward-thinking moves. He owned a corner lot in Northeast Philly, the same property where the family lived. But instead of seeing it as just a home, he saw it as a foundation for expansion. He subdivided the lot and began construction on a second home next door. It was his first personal development project, built with cash flow, credit, and gut instinct.

But before construction ever broke ground, something happened that shook the family's sense of security.

A man from the UK first walked into Hanavi's world as a customer, buying a car off the lot. He had charm, an easy manner, and a story about starting fresh in the States with his young daughter. One sale turned into longer conversations, the kind that hint at more than small talk. Maybe he mentioned wanting to invest; maybe there was talk of partnering on something bigger. We'll never know the exact words exchanged, but if you knew Hanavi, you knew every invitation had a reason. Even when emotion steered the wheel, calculation was under the hood.

When the man and his daughter came to dinner, it didn't feel out of place, it felt like the start of something. Trust was being built. Then, on a random afternoon as the kids were returning from school, that trust shattered. The FBI swarmed the house, front door, backyard, all sides. Agents in windbreakers and unmarked cars. The man had abducted his daughter from her mother overseas. Just like that, a federal case was in Hanavi's living room. It rattled the walls, but not his nature. Even in chaos, his instinct to open the door, to explore an opportunity, never left. It just learned to look harder at who was knocking.

Once the second house was completed on the subdivided lot, it became an immediate asset. Family members who visited were hosted there, and later, it was leased, another stream in Hanavi's growing network of cash flow and control.

By 1995, another transition was brewing, this time to Cherry Hill, New Jersey. The home sat at the edge of a quiet cul-de-sac on nearly an acre of land. A long walkway led to a four-columned porch, and inside, a spiral staircase curled toward the second floor beneath a hanging chandelier. Painted bright white with classic colonial lines, the mailbox read La Casa Blanca. It wasn't the grandest estate in town, but to the family, it was the White House.

Cherry Hill was a declaration. Hanavi was no longer just surviving. He was staging. A bigger house. A stronger district. A louder message.

It was around this time that Hanavi's father passed away.

He wasn't able to attend the funeral. The burial took place in Israel, carried out by his siblings and family still living there. Hanavi grieved from afar, but as always, he found a way to be part of it. He sent money to help cover the expenses, just as he had done many times before. Those contributions weren't just acts of support, they were declarations of value.

When Hanavi gave, he didn't just feel generous. He felt seen. Providing for his siblings made him feel accomplished. Respected. The brother who had made it.

The family didn't mourn loudly. Hanavi didn't cry in front of anyone. But something inside him changed after that.

He was never a religious man, never kept strict observance, never followed every law. But he held deep reverence for tradition. He made sure the proper prayers were said. That the burial followed Jewish law. That his father's memory would be honored, even if not enshrined in ritual.

Respect, to Hanavi, was a form of faith.

In the months surrounding his father's death, maybe even just before it, Hanavi began looking for strength in places he hadn't explored before. It wasn't religion in the way most people think of it. He never put on tefillin each morning or started keeping kosher with precision. But something about Kabbalah called to him. Not the mysticism alone, but the promise, whether real or imagined, that if you studied deeply enough, believed strongly enough, and aligned yourself with the patterns of the universe, the world might bend in your favor.

For Hanavi, Kabbalah wasn't a scholarly pursuit. It was a private playbook. A source of spiritual leverage. Maybe it carried the promise of clarity, maybe even of financial freedom, an invisible architecture for the life he still wanted to build. Or maybe that's just what he told himself in the quiet moments, when grief and ambition met in the same breath.

After the funeral, he didn't talk about legacy the same way. His tone shifted. Real estate wasn't just property anymore. It was permanence. A way to outlast mortality.

And that's when his eyes turned fully to Olde City Philadelphia.

The buildings there were old, cracked at the edges, but filled with story. Brick facades, iron railings, corner lots near history itself. It was perfect. Hanavi began to see the city not as it was, but as it could be. Boutique shops. Mixed-use buildings. Hidden courtyards. Real estate became more than a business. It became how he processed loss. How he coped with control slipping, first from his father's hands, and someday, inevitably, from his own.

Cherry Hill wasn't just where life got bigger.

It was where time started to feel more finite.

Chapter 5:
Leveraged Hands

By the spring of 1998, Hanavi was already plotting his next play.

He didn't say it outright. He rarely did. But his movements always betrayed him. The mechanic's days were long behind him, as was the cab. Manual labor had been a rite of passage, a chapter written in sweat and speed, then closed without sentiment.

Now, he lived in maneuvering, deals over handshakes, leverage drawn from perception, moves designed to be seen as much as they were meant to succeed.

The way he dressed had shifted, linen shirts pressed flat, shoes shined, cuffs sharpened. He walked into rooms as if he already owned them.

That year, when his eldest son turned eighteen, Hanavi did something that seemed almost magnanimous.

He handed over a property in Olde City, a narrow storefront wedged between art galleries and loft spaces. Once, in the 1970s, it had been a leather goods distribution center. Decades later it still smelled faintly of treated hide, dust, and the mustiness of inventory that hadn't moved in years. Stacks of belts with cracked leather, boxes of goods still wearing faded tags, shelves sagging from neglect.

Hanavi stood in the center of the space, running a hand over one of the wooden counters.

"This is yours to run," he told his son.

The shop was overhauled, new shelving, fresh paint, a modern register. The front window was cleaned until it shone, reflecting the brick-and-stone rhythm of the block. On paper, it was the son's business. But Hanavi's presence was still woven into every detail. Contractors stopped by weekly to "check on things" and collect what he called petty cash. He didn't need to explain the arrangement. The son understood, this was a gift, but it came tethered to his father's grip.

It was enough. The son worked the space, learned the rhythms of inventory and customers, and kept the loyalty that Hanavi valued above any profit margin.

By the end of the following year, the horizon shifted.

In the fall of 1999, Hanavi uprooted the family to Miami.

They didn't just relocate, they arrived. First-class tickets, a limousine idling at the airport curb, palm trees swaying in humid air that smelled faintly of salt and jet fuel.

The new house had oversized windows that caught the light, floors so polished they seemed to hum underfoot. From certain angles, it might have looked like the water was just beyond the hedges. Hanavi never confirmed it. Ambiguity was part of the image.

But Philadelphia was not yet in the rearview.

There were still properties, partnerships, and connections that needed tending. Every few weeks, he and his eldest son flew back north. The trips became a ritual: coffee at the airport, a quiet drive through familiar streets, inspections of buildings and deals, collecting what was owed.

Then came the morning that ritual broke.

They landed in Philadelphia as usual. The air was sharp with early cold. They drove to the office Hanavi had co-owned for years, a corner space that had been both a base of operations and a place where his reputation lived in the walls. He stepped to the door, turned the key.

It didn't fit.

He tried again. Same resistance. He frowned, jiggled the lock, tried the spare.

Still nothing.

For a moment, he blamed the mechanics of the lock, or the weather swelling the doorframe. But as he looked closer, at the polished new hardware, the freshly painted frame, understanding spread like ice.

The locks had been changed.

His name removed.

Inside, the furniture was gone, the phones disconnected, the hum of that place erased.

No warning. No conversation. Just erasure.

He called. The line rang. No answer. The voicemail tone hit, and his voice, sharp, unfiltered, thundered down the line. It started as controlled fury, but quickly broke into something more primal, words collapsing into growls and half-breathed syllables. Betrayal doesn't always roar, it can splinter, cracking the voice of a man who has spent decades believing no one could take the game from him.

His son stood beside him on the sidewalk, silent. Watching a man who had built his life on never being cornered face a door that refused him entry.

Hanavi didn't linger. He pivoted.

The office was gone, the partnership finished, the trust dissolved. There was nothing to negotiate.

If this was how it ended, cold and cowardly, then he would end it louder.

Within weeks, every Philadelphia asset was liquidated, transferred, or left behind.

The bridges weren't just burned, they were reduced to ash.

Back in Miami, he threw himself deeper into his projects. Construction crews rotated in and out, cars were flipped for profit, small developments sprang up in different corners of the city. His eldest son was drawn closer into the machinery, managing job sites, dealing with contractors, holding the clipboard instead of the keys.

But the lines were clear. The reins were long, never loose.

Hanavi had built everything on instinct and control, and that control wasn't something he handed over, not to partners, not to blood.

In his mind, the lockout wasn't just a warning.

It was proof that legacy couldn't be shared too soon.

And in the game as he played it, he was still the dealer.

Still holding the cards.

No one else got to play the final hand.

Chapter 6:
Breaking Point

The locks had changed in Philly, but Hanavi didn't flinch in Miami.

He returned not as a man defeated, but as a man reborn. And the first order of business wasn't court filings or damage control.

It was remodeling.

The house, already impressive, was transformed. He tore up every trace of what had come before. Marble flooring, imported, wall to wall. Floor-to-ceiling Venetian plaster in every room, giving the walls a sheen that seemed to reflect motion itself. Additional bathrooms were added with precision. Fixtures replaced. Corners sharpened.

The backyard became a sanctuary: expanded patio, rebuilt columns, updated landscaping, and enough space for a gathering of thirty, or one powerful moment of solitude. The message was clear:

"We're not just here. We're staying."

He didn't build a home. He crafted a statement.

Inside, his wife ran the operations like a seasoned general, maids, meals, laundry, hospitality, order. She made sure the place felt like it matched its presentation.

When guests came, they weren't simply visiting, they were checking into what friends and family half-joked, half-meant when they called it The Hotel Hanavi. It wasn't just a house;

it was an all-inclusive experience. Guests had warm, private rooms with beds that felt like home, three full meals a day, and every amenity one could imagine, fresh linens, a stocked fridge, strong coffee in the morning, fine wine in the evening, and cigars for those who shared his taste. Mornings began with the smell of fresh bread or cardamom coffee drifting through the hallways. Evenings carried the slow, rich aroma of stews and roasted meats.

No matter how long they stayed, visitors were absorbed into the household's rhythm. They were part of the table talk, the late-night laughter, the carefully orchestrated sense that here, at least, the outside world could not touch them. For a weekend or a month, life at The Hotel Hanavi was a curated paradise.

Hanavi was the host in the spotlight. His wife was the quiet conductor behind the scenes. Together, they made sure no one ever left feeling like a guest, they left feeling like they'd lived in a rare, private world.

The living room was redesigned around a single item: a brand-new Grand television, the largest on the market at the time. Heavy. Bulky. Bold. He didn't order it for delivery. He drove to a trusted consumer electronics dealer in the heart of Miami and picked it up himself. That TV was installed the same day, mounted like a throne.

He paired it with the Israeli network and a newly installed surround sound system that made every broadcast feel like a homecoming. Sitting in his chair, coffee or cigar in hand, his kingdom wrapped around him, digital, architectural, domestic.

He had lost ground in Philadelphia, but here?

He was immovable.

Yet beneath the marble and media systems, the strain was growing.

The legal battles in Philadelphia didn't go away. They multiplied. Every court date drained him, not just financially, but psychologically. Partners flipped. Assets were sold under duress. Equity was swallowed by settlements. He played it off in Miami with the same charm that once made him magnetic. But he was bleeding, quietly.

The liquidity crisis trickled into his new life.

Then, September 11th, 2001.

The towers fell.

The economy froze.

Deals collapsed. Lenders vanished. Capital ran cold. And Hanavi, usually ahead of the curve, found himself scrambling. Real estate stopped moving. Construction stalled. Investors pulled out. He watched the news unfold from that same 60-inch screen, hands clenched, eyes locked. He didn't speak. Not for a while.

But motion was his medicine.

If the world tightened, he expanded.

He restructured deals, spun panic into opportunity, leaned on seller-financing strategies and peer capital to keep the engines warm. And to his community? He was thriving. He sponsored events, showed up in newsletters, supported synagogues and fundraisers, and mentored up-and-comers who clung to his every word.

In Miami, he was a pillar.

People came to him for advice, favors, capital, referrals. He was the man who made you believe anything was still possible. They didn't know about the overnight court filings. They didn't know about the bridge loans used to patch the fallout of failed Philly ventures.

They didn't see the hemorrhage.

They saw the house.

They saw the marble.

They saw the plasma screen.

They saw the lion.

Chapter 7:
Let It Ride

The first sign wasn't a failed deal.

It was his face.

One morning, something was off. The left side of his mouth didn't move quite right. His smile was uneven. His words, usually crisp and commanding, came out slightly muddled, like they had to fight their way out.

It was his wife who noticed first.

She tilted her head as he spoke and narrowed her eyes, not with fear, but with familiarity. She had been watching closely, even as he insisted, he was fine.

When the slurring got worse, she didn't ask permission.

She took him to the hospital.

There, doctors confirmed it: Bell's Palsy. Temporary, maybe. Stress-induced, almost certainly. It wasn't a stroke, they said, but it was a warning. A flashing red light on the dashboard he refused to acknowledge.

Still, even in the hospital, he made phone calls. Asked for documents. Made jokes to the nurses. Tried to control the room like it was a board meeting.

"Just another muscle refusing to listen," he said.

But something in his voice, slower, quieter, betrayed the truth.

By now, his reach spanned far beyond Miami.

He had flips and partnerships across Upstate New York, Florida's coasts, Oklahoma, Alabama, anywhere a distressed asset whispered potential, Hanavi was there. If it had a tax lien, a foreclosure filing, or a widow ready to sell fast, he circled it.

He had attorneys on retainer in multiple states, watching due diligence like hawks, writing addenda at midnight, preparing for the worst so he could chase the best. But those retainers weren't cheap.

Neither was the lifestyle.

Hanavi still drove luxury. Hosted exclusive parties with hired entertainers flown in last minute. Paid for every lunch, no exceptions. Guests were invited to join him on his yacht docked in a private marina. He didn't just attend events, he funded them, sponsored them, and was often the reason they happened.

To the outside world, he was untouchable.

To the spreadsheet, he was break-even on a good day.

The books were volatile. There were weeks where five-figure checks cleared and weeks where payroll came out of a line of credit. But no one saw that.

They saw the swagger.

They saw the boat.

They saw the lunch bill.

The button-down shirt opened one notch too far, the jewelry, the scent of cigar smoke and confidence that made you believe he owned the block, even if the books said otherwise.

They saw the wave.

Not the undertow.

One project almost brought light back into the chaos.

It was a multifamily complex in Oklahoma, purchased at a discount just before Hurricane Katrina devastated New Orleans in 2005. When evacuees needed housing, Hanavi pivoted.

He turned the property into temporary relief housing, offering reduced rent and compassion-laced leases. For a moment, the spotlight was soft and warm. Local coverage praised the effort. He walked the property with dignity, chest out, eyes sharper than they had been in weeks.

But goodwill isn't good business without good management.

And Hanavi was managing from 1,200 miles away. He eventually flew a friend out to take over management and control of the property, but much of the damage was already done. The tenants had looted and destroyed what had begun as a goodwill business decision.

Within months, problems emerged. Units were damaged. Tenants didn't pay. Partners went silent. The management firm he relied on turned out to be both understaffed and underqualified. City inspectors wrote violations. Expenses ballooned.

Quietly, he sold the asset.

Another mark on the scoreboard. Not a win. Not a total loss. Just another round gone sideways.

Back in Miami, even as the tension mounted and the wear showed beneath the surface, the invitations never stopped.

There were still Friday night dinners, lavish and loud, holidays with always an abundance of guests to entertain. The home was always open, warm, and welcoming. Regardless of the internal financial depravity, Hanavi somehow always pulled a rabbit out of his hat.

Still yacht outings with handpicked guests and clinking glasses. Still weekday lunches where he covered the bill before it hit the table. If anything, he leaned in harder. He had to be seen, felt, heard.

Being unavailable was never an option.

He didn't skip events, he curated them.

He didn't retreat, he hosted.

He remained in the pilot seat, eyes forward, voice steady.

Deals were still closing. Documents still crossed his desk. Phones still rang, and he still answered.

He wasn't absent.

He was everywhere.

Even when he was tired, he never let the room see it. That was the unspoken rule: you don't get tired when you're the engine.

But the engine was running hot.

The blueprints were still fresh, but the cracks had already begun. What once soared with vision now staggered with silence. And the man who built futures was quietly negotiating with the collapse of his own.

Still, on Friday nights, the house lit up like a festival.

The table groaned under platters of roasted lamb, bowls of bright salads, braided challah still warm from the oven. Children darted between the chairs while grown men leaned back, telling the kind of stories that start with a laugh and end with a sigh. Hanavi presided over it all, pouring wine with the same flourish he used to sign contracts, his voice booming over the clatter of forks and the rise of song.

On those nights, you could believe nothing was wrong. That the man at the head of the table was exactly as untouchable as he appeared.

But in the quiet after the guests left, when the last candle hissed out and the house settled into a hush, you could almost hear the weight in his footsteps as he walked down the hall. He lingered in the doorway of his study, staring at a skyline he'd never built, imagining the towers, the deals, the permanence he still believed were just one move away.

Because for Hanavi, there was always one more play. One more shot at something bigger, something that would outlast him.

He didn't know it yet, but the cards for that bet were already on the table. And this time, the stakes wouldn't just be the deal.

They would be everything.

Chapter 8:
All-In, No Exit

By 2006, Hanavi wasn't just stacking wins; he was building something that could outlast the noise. When his eldest married that year, the celebration was staged at a prominent hall in Aventura, crystal light pooling over white tablecloths and a band pulsing through the room. He didn't fly in florals or exotic centerpieces. He did something more intentional, he made sure the neighborhood itself was threaded into the evening. Caterers, decorators, printers, limo guys, even the man who had once rushed a banner hours before Shabbat, everyone who had a business in the community had a piece of his celebration. To be there was to be inside his orbit.

Outside, under the porte cochère, the white Rolls-Royce Phantom idled like punctuation at the end of a long sentence. But that sentence started years earlier. He'd always been chasing a feeling he couldn't quite buy: the Bentley Continental that looked right but sat wrong, the Cadillac Escalade with presence but no voltage, the Mercedes S500 that nearly quieted the hunger and somehow didn't. The truth was simple and a little dangerous, he needed the desire alive to keep chasing the cash flow that fed the image, not the other way around.

The itch went back further still. In Israel he'd owned a stubborn little box of a car he nicknamed "Pushme", Dah-fu-ni, likely a Susita, all angles and problems, the most consistent of which was that it needed a running start. He'd laugh and wave a cousin over to help, then coast it into first like a magician. Even then, the car wasn't metal; it was a promise. One day, nothing he drove would need pushing.

The Phantom delivered that promise in pearl paint and cream leather, white wool underfoot, the Spirit of Ecstasy pointing him forward. For a few hours that night, with Israeli music swelling and the room moving as one, he wasn't performing legacy, he was it.

But the air was already changing, and he could feel it if he stood still long enough. The ads for pre-construction condos were multiplying while the buyers grew picky. Appraisers began to hedge. Lenders who once spoke in exclamation points started calling with questions that sounded like warnings. It was only hints then, paper fraying at the edges, but the edges were everywhere.

That fall, he set his eyes on a piece of dirt with a view that made men promise things: a bayside parcel, correct zoning, raw potential. He called it Vista Del Cielo because that's what it felt like in the renderings, the city rising to meet the sky. At that stage, it was foreshadowing more than fact: sketches pinned to foam board, a sales deck with sunlit elevations, glass turned into possibility by a good printer. He'd leased an office, took meetings there because the chairs matched the pitch, but the move into the on-site trailer, the daily theatre, wouldn't come until much later, only after the signatures made it real.

An investor surfaced, warm money, not hot; the kind that sits quiet in escrow while a better exit is hunted. It wasn't unusual in his world. Hanavi had a signature move when the numbers allowed it: get in early, shop the upside, flip the paper, move on. He was good at it not because he loved the flip, but because his investors loved that he could make one happen. Their strategy was clean: place a bet, let Hanavi find the bigger fish, then pull out and count the vig of relief. If the wind shifted, they could always say they were never fully in, just visiting.

By late spring 2007, the wind did shift. Submarkets that used to hum went quiet. A couple of banks changed their tone mid-conversation. You could smell caution the way you can smell rain in old masonry, the trailer would carry that scent later, but even the leased office picked it up in the carpet and in the silence after the phone calls. Then came the call from the investor's attorney. The words were soft; the meaning wasn't.

"We're stepping aside," he said.

The escrow, everyone's favorite halfway house for commitment, had done its job. Park the money, hold the place, wait for Hanavi to conjure a clean flip, and if the sky darkens, lift the anchor. Pull out. That was the risk embedded in every handshake: the exit was a feature, not a failure.

He chased replacements from Aventura to New York, then farther, private funds, family offices, anyone whose courage hadn't curdled yet. Most wanted renderings and comps and then asked a quiet question with their eyes: What if the music really is stopping?

The answer came in an office that smelled like leather and newly opened envelopes. The lender didn't care for poetry or skyline dreams.

"More," he said. "Everything."

Everything meant everything that was a mentionable asset on his personal financial statement, plus whatever else he could leverage, house, personal guarantees, the remaining cars, lines he'd sworn he'd never cross. Even his lawyer winced. "This doesn't protect you," he said. "It exposes you."

Hanavi signed anyway. Not because he didn't see the cliff, but because stepping back now would turn every dollar he'd put down into a headstone. After closing, only after closing, he moved into the trailer. Glass walls, a foldout site plan, a cigar in a box atop his desk, and a presence he wore like a tailored suit. The smell of old masonry hung in the heat, mineral and memory, as if the ground itself remembered other men who had tried to raise their names against the sky.

By late 2008, the bridge loan hit maturity. He'd built in interest reserves, carved a small cash-out for soft costs, and floated the operation as long as the numbers let him. On paper, it worked; in the world, it didn't. Buyers vanished. The reserves thinned to a thread. Vista Del Cielo, once a foreshadowing that felt like fate, stalled, then went still.

The selling began, the yacht, the collection, even the Phantom. He kept moving, because movement was the one currency he still controlled. When someone would ask if he was stepping back, he'd give a tired half-smile.

"Still in the game," he'd say. And then, because it was true, because it had always been true, he'd add, "It's only money." He knew how to make money. That formula was not foreign to him. What he couldn't make was time, or wind, or a market that had stopped believing in glass.

He locked the trailer one evening after a meeting that didn't go anywhere, turned the cigar box so the hinge faced the wall, and walked the length of the temporary ramp slowly. The sky over the bay had that late-hour color that makes every unfinished thing ache. Tomorrow would require a different kind of courage, quieter and meaner, the kind that doesn't announce itself with a car or a lobby. Tomorrow, the calls he'd take would not be about views.

And that is where the next chapter begins.

Chapter 9:
Down to the Felt

When the dust finally settled in late 2008, Hanavi wasn't out of the game.

He was cornered, but alive.

The bridge loan had matured. The funds had dried. The project had gone dark. Investors had gone quiet. But every morning, he still put on the armor, pressed shirt, polished shoes, fresh shave, and walked out the door like he had somewhere important to be.

Because in his mind, he did.

Vista Del Cielo may have collapsed, but Hanavi hadn't. Not yet.

He still believed he could salvage it.

If not as a tower, then as a flip. A packaged asset. A distressed opportunity for someone with capital and the nerve to use it. The land was still zoned. The permits, though stale, had once been near final. The vision still lived in his chest like a second heartbeat. If he couldn't build it, maybe he could pass the torch for a piece of the flame.

He took meetings wherever he could find them, coffee shops, hotel lobbies, borrowed conference rooms. But in his mind, the meeting would still take place in the trailer as long as he had access. If the trailer was alive, so was the deal. And if the deal was alive, so was he.

He brought his plans in a leather folio now, not spread across glass tables. He pitched in fragments, calibrated to each listener:

We've got pre-development done. The city's already warmed up to it. The permits were almost through. It's turnkey if you just inject the capital.

Some listened out of politeness. Most didn't.

Even the deepest pockets balked. The numbers didn't work. The exposure was too high. No one wanted to inherit someone else's cliff.

But Hanavi didn't stop.

Retreat wasn't in his wiring. Even as the margin for error shrank and the calls thinned, he pushed forward. Not because he couldn't see the odds, but because belief was the only currency he had left.

His oldest son saw the toll.

He watched his father come home later, slower. Still dressed sharp, but with a different kind of silence in his voice, the kind that follows a meeting that ends with We'll be in touch when everyone knows they won't.

By then, the son was a husband, and now a father himself.

In 2008, Hanavi became a grandfather.

A boy. Healthy. Wide-eyed. Born into a family trying to recalibrate what "legacy" really meant.

For the first time, the son stopped looking to the family business for footing.

There was no extra household budget. No handouts. No promises.

He stepped out quietly and went to work elsewhere, not because he lost respect, but because he gained responsibility. Feeding his own family mattered more than chasing what might have been.

And Hanavi understood, even if he didn't say it aloud.

Still, he moved.

He took calls daily. Scanned for deals. Tried to reposition old assets into new conversations. Lawyers. Brokers. Old buyers. New whispers.

Hope hadn't left him.

But time… time was becoming louder.

Deals moved slower. Options thinner. And the home, his last true stronghold, began to creak under the pressure.

Still, he held it together.

Because there was a new life in the world. A grandson.

A new name to carry the line.

And in Hanavi's mind, that meant there was still work to do.

Failure didn't send Hanavi home, it sent him elsewhere.

A friend of a friend had a connection: a high-floor penthouse office suite in a professional complex nearby had just opened up. The view wasn't the bay, but it faced the city, still wide, still open. The previous tenant had defaulted. The space was dusty, bare, but affordable, especially with the right negotiation.

Hanavi didn't hesitate. He needed to show he was still breathing and in charge. He needed a change of location, a shift in ground, somewhere he could stand and say he still had footing.

He kept a corner suite for himself, outfitted with heavy antique wood furniture. He had no interest in the modern minimalism of a glass desk; he preferred weight, history, presence. In the corner sat an antique sidebar he had acquired through another venture opportunity, a reminder of the multifaceted routes he had taken to flip a dollar, even when real estate itself was at a halt. He never halted.

The rest of the floor, he carved into smaller offices.

Not as a landlord, but as a survivalist.

Small firms. Immigrant attorneys. Startup agents. Anyone who needed a desk and a door. He divided the space into zones and collected monthly rent, slowly building a cash-flow cushion, or at least maximizing some relief from the liability he had taken on.

It wasn't glamorous.

But it was his.

Every morning, he returned to a new kind of routine. Shirt pressed. Coffee hot. Keys in hand. He drove to that office like it was a high-rise in Manhattan.

When he arrived, he walked the halls, checked in on tenants, printed prospectuses, and reworked old deals with new numbers.

To the few who came through, it looked like a modest hub.

To Hanavi?

It was the next bet.

Quiet. Steady. Real.

This time, there were no blueprints. No cranes. No need to promise towers in the sky.

Just foot traffic. Rent checks. Phone calls. Hustle.

It wasn't legacy yet, but it was motion.

And for Hanavi, motion always meant hope.

Chapter 10:
Drawing Dead

By 2010, the remnants of Hanavi's empire were scattered, small real estate deals, whispered lawsuits, and unpaid debts that loomed like clouds no one acknowledged but everyone felt. His calls still came with confidence, his entrances still carried weight. But the world around him had changed. And slowly, the world stopped answering back.

The name that once opened doors now raised eyebrows. Contacts who once begged to buy in were suddenly too busy. Bankers who once praised him now demanded everything in writing. He was no longer the architect of opportunity; he was a man chasing echoes.

And in truth, the architecture of the game itself had shifted. The way investors and banks had traditionally managed risk was no longer the same. The old rules, where relationships could bridge the gap between paper and trust, where collateral could be "massaged" into acceptability, where time was a negotiable currency, were giving way to a new rigidity. In the wake of the financial crisis, risk was no longer something you could charm away. Underwriting had hardened. Capital had become cautious. Even the sharks were circling slower, calculating more, biting less. The handshakes and late-night deals that once greased the system were being replaced by layers of compliance, audit trails, and an almost surgical demand for proof. For a man who had built his life on instinct and momentum, this wasn't just a shift in the rules, it was a change in the terrain itself.

Still, he performed the part. His style never changed: an easy, open-collared shirt, jeans, and soft loafers, casual, but intentional. It wasn't flash. It was freedom. He wore comfort like armor, as if to say, I'm still my own man.

He told stories over coffee in diners that once welcomed him like a king. Scribbled new deals on napkins as if the pen held magic. But it wasn't magic anymore, it was muscle memory.

And then came the solitude.

Some days, he wouldn't leave the house. Other days, he'd be out for hours with no clear destination. When asked where he had been, he'd wave it off with a familiar grin. "Just making moves."

But the moves were shrinking. The circles smaller. His breath shorter. His back tighter. Yet he told no one. He held pain like he held secrets, with clenched teeth and straight posture.

There was a small bodega in the office complex below, and he made it part of his ritual. Almost daily, he'd walk down, grab a chocolate treat, something sweet but simple, and a lottery ticket. It wasn't about the odds. It was about the hope. A quiet prayer wrapped in foil and numbers. That maybe today was the day it all turned around.

He kept an office suite in the building long after there was any business to conduct there. It wasn't about utility. It was about identity. That office was the last battleground where he was still "in the game." Leasing out parts of the space gave the illusion of motion and provided a small trickle of cash flow, but the office itself was his anchor.

One deal still lingered. A small, distressed multifamily property, old connection, new opportunity. He read the offer twice. Not because it was complex, but because he wanted to believe again. He reached for his humidor, pulled out a Romeo y Julieta, and stepped outside.

Tommy Bahama shirt untucked. Loafers broken in. He drew slow. Let the cigar burn like memory. His silhouette blurred in the patio light, part smoke, part survival.

"Still in the game," he whispered.

But even he knew. The game had changed. And the playbook? There wasn't one.

No passwords. No asset list. No succession plan. Just scribbles in notebooks and ideas never handed off.

The legacy was locked in motion.

And motion doesn't pass down, it disappears.

What he didn't say, what we never asked, became the silence we inherited.

BODEGA

Chapter 11:
The Illusion of Control

From the outside, Hanavi still carried himself like a man who owned the ground beneath his feet. But time had begun to leave its mark—not in the flash of his clothes, which no longer needed announcing, but in the way he held his frame. The upright, commanding stance that once drew eyes across a room now carried a slight forward lean, as if gravity had quietly won a negotiation. Shoulders, once squared like a prizefighter's, had settled lower, and when he walked, the stride was shorter, deliberate, more measured—like each step had to be accounted for before it landed.

The ritual walks to the bodega continued, though slower. A pause at the curb. A hand on the doorframe before stepping in. He still greeted the clerk with that half-smile that said I'm still here, bought his chocolate and lottery ticket, and left with the same nod he'd given for years. To a passerby, nothing had changed. But if you watched closely, you'd see the pauses were longer, the breath heavier, the return walk home more of a journey than a stroll.

Behind closed doors, the cracks showed. He leaned on medication—not recklessly, but with the quiet dependency of someone who knew the relief was temporary and took it anyway. Sleep became his truest escape, more comfortable than the sharp awareness of his body's quiet betrayals.

The superstition about men in his family not living past a certain age had been with him for decades. Now, as he drifted closer to that invisible line, it didn't spur him to outrun it—

it made him want to choreograph his approach. If it had to come, it would meet him while he was still at the wheel.

Then the second stroke arrived—not as a lightning bolt, but as a slow leak. Pauses in conversation. Moments where his gaze hung just a fraction too long before returning. The words that used to fire off without hesitation now stumbled, looking for the right doorway out. When the family suggested a hospital, he cut them off—sharp, defensive:

"What do you know? I'm fine."

He wasn't.

The ambulance came. The hospital confirmed it. A stent was placed. There was a new regimen of pills and warnings. He nodded through the discharge like it was a business negotiation he intended to win, not a surrender to circumstances.

But when he stepped back into the house—a house he had personally shaped and claimed for more than two decades— he stopped cold in the entryway. His eyes swept the space as if he'd never seen it before.

"This isn't my house," he said flatly.

He pointed at the front door he had installed himself years ago and insisted it was a replacement. Claimed the television wasn't the same. That the furniture had been moved. That someone had sold the house and rebuilt a copy.

It wasn't anger in his voice. It was disorientation. Fear.

Some details, oddly, weren't wrong. The television had been replaced. A chair had been shifted. But the foundation was unchanged—it was his memory that had drifted, unmoored from its anchor points.

For the family, it was a shiver down the spine.

In those hours after the stroke, a new fear took root—not just for his health, but for what his incapacity meant. There was no will. No power of attorney. No written instructions. Just a house full of obligations, memories, and open questions.

What if he didn't come back from this?

But the fog lifted, at least enough for him to function. And as quickly as the urgency had arrived, it faded. The hard conversations—about plans, permissions, protection— slipped back into the shadows.

Because maybe there was nothing left to protect. The empire was long gone. The house was leveraged. The legacy, everyone realized, had never been built into something that could stand without him.

For years, they had believed something solid was being shaped behind the chaos. That beneath the moves and the noise, there was a vault, a blueprint, a safety net.

There wasn't.

There was only the man—a man who had lived with force, built with instinct, and convinced himself that control was a permanent possession.

And now, standing in his own home with a lottery ticket in one hand and a memory that slipped like sand through the other, Hanavi did the only thing he knew:

He kept playing.

Because stopping would mean admitting the game had ended.

Chapter 12:
Dead Man's Hand

By the time his walk changed, it was no longer subtle. Hanavi moved with hesitation, stiff-legged, his steps short and deliberate, like each motion came at the cost of something internal. And he wasn't quiet about it anymore. He groaned getting up. Cursed the ache in his bones. Pleaded aloud for someone to bring him medication "something strong." Sometimes the pain made him shout. Other times, he simply wanted to be comforted.

His wife did what she could. She was with him day and night. Helping him dress. Helping him eat. Adjusting him when he slid in his chair. But this was beyond one person. It was no longer just aging—it was deterioration.

Still, he resisted going to the hospital. Always had.

Then the signs became visible.

His toe had turned black. Hardened. Cold. The infection had already begun. The tissue was dying. Gangrene had set in.

It was the kind of damage that doesn't happen overnight. Years of unmanaged diabetes had been quietly working beneath the surface—narrowing his blood vessels, dulling the nerves in his feet, cutting off sensation. When you can't feel the pain of a small cut or sore, it festers. Circulation slows. Healing stalls. And in time, infection takes over. In his case, by the time anyone could convince him to look, the tissue had already crossed the point of no return.

No matter how obvious the condition, he refused help. Said he didn't need a hospital. Said it would pass. Said just give him a minute.

But two people finally got through to him—not family, not doctors. Just a man and a woman, both familiar faces who had been quietly helping him for years. They weren't a couple. They weren't paid. They weren't obligated. They simply showed up.

They picked up cigars when he called. Ran errands without question. Gave him rides, sat with him, waited patiently through his moods and commands. At first, his family didn't trust them. Everyone around Hanavi seemed to have an angle.

But over time, it became clear: they didn't.

That day, they stopped by again. They saw his condition. They saw the foot. And they didn't ask—they told him it was time to go.

And for some reason, he agreed.

Just as they were walking him out—slowly, supporting his arms, guiding him toward the car—his son pulled into the driveway, home from work. The door was open. Hanavi was on the threshold. Not in control, not issuing commands just letting someone else take the lead for once.

It was a strange image to take in.

He had refused help for weeks. And now, he was letting them take him.

At the hospital, the news came fast.

The toe was beyond saving. Most of the foot, too.

They had to amputate.

Only his wife was called in as the primary contact. The rest of the family remained by phone—alert, anxious, on standby. Updates were relayed in pieces. She carried the weight of it in real time.

After surgery, the doctors came back with more.

Scans showed that the infection had traveled further than expected. They would have to amputate below the knee.

Hanavi was still unconscious. He didn't yet know what he had lost only that more was coming.

His wife called the children. She needed to tell them what the doctors said. What they wanted to do next. Everyone gave input. But in the end, the hospital needed a signature.

And it was hers to give.

She signed.

Then came the next truth: Hanavi had signed a DNR.

A Do Not Resuscitate order. It was already on file.

If things went wrong, he didn't want to be revived. No breathing machines. No chest compressions. No ventilators.

It wasn't a question. It was a decision he had made long ago.

He survived the operation.

And with survival came the weight of what could be. There was still a light ahead—a truth that many people not only live with prosthetics but thrive with them. Technology could offer him a chance at movement again, at a life beyond the chair. Therapists spoke of progress, of possibility. In their eyes, he still had a road forward.

But Hanavi had never been a man content to be managed. He was a lion who had lived his life in the wild, unbound and unruled. He didn't want to be tamed—didn't want to be trained into a smaller version of himself, measured by careful steps on parallel bars. The reality was setting in: even with the best equipment, he would not return to the man who once moved like a force of nature.

Long before this, in a moment we all thought was just bravado, he had said that if he were ever crippled, his existence should end. It was a harsh statement, but it wasn't drama it was his reality. To him, life was only worth living if it was lived on his terms: fast, loud, unrestrained.

When warned about cigars, about sugar, about exercise, he'd wave it off with a smirk and say, "What do I have left?" The words carried more than defiance they were his quiet admission that the will to carry on was not rooted in longevity, but in liberty. And now, sitting in the shadow of that hospital stay, those words weren't just a quip. They were the compass he was already following.

He tried to learn how to walk again. Went to the appointments. Got fitted for a prosthetic. Met with therapists.

But the pressure was unbearable. The prosthetic bruised. The wound never quite closed. And then came the phantom pain a limb that wasn't there still screaming back at him.

He fell. Repeatedly.

The living room. The bathroom. The hall.

Each time, it was harder to get him up.

He gave up on the prosthetic and chose the wheelchair. It was easier. Less painful.

But it meant he stopped trying.

And the burden shifted entirely to his wife.

She became his full-time caregiver. No nurses. No staff. Just her.

She lifted him, cleaned him, clothed him, steadied him. She changed bandages. Kept track of appointments. Listened to the groans at night and held his arm when he broke down.

They assumed insurance would cover more.

It didn't.

A brief window of in-home support followed hospitalization, but it was short-lived and insufficient. And after that, the help disappeared leaving not just the physical work, but the emotional strain to pile on.

One of the assigned therapists who came to see him at home didn't know what he was walking into. On the surface, the sessions were about strength, balance, and recovery. But in conversation, Hanavi caught a detail — the man was Cuban. That was all it took.

He leaned in, casual but calculated, steering the dialogue with questions until the truth came out: the therapist had access to Cuban cigars. Not just any Romeo y Julietas, the exact kind Hanavi had always favored. From there, the therapy sessions took on a different rhythm. Between stretches and exercises, there were gentle nudges, shared laughs, a slow weaving of charm and relentless, pleasant persistence.

By the time those few sessions were over, two boxes had arrived at the house. Hanavi may have lost his footing, but when he saw something he wanted, the old instincts never failed him. The hunt, the negotiation, the seal of the deal — they kicked in like second nature. Even in a wheelchair, even in pain, he could still close.

He made calls late at night. Not to family but to old friends. Old associates. Names from the poker tables and property deals. People he once flew across the country to meet.

"Bring me something," he'd say. "Please. I need it. Just help me sleep."

Most didn't answer.

Some gave promises and never followed through.

The circle had shrunk. The power was gone. His world had quieted.

But one person never left.

His wife.

She stayed. Through it all. Not because she had to—but because she saw the man inside the broken frame.

She remembered him before the chair. Before the losses. Before the noise went quiet. She stayed. Because that's what love does when the world turns its back.

It keeps showing up.

DO NOT RESUSCITATE
AMPUTATION

Chapter 13:
All In

The wheelchair was never supposed to be part of the story.

Hanavi made that bitterly clear one afternoon, after a friend of his wife brought her husband over for a short visit. The man was in a wheelchair—frail, friendly, fading.

After they left, Hanavi scoffed with venom:

"If I ever end up like that, just pull the plug."

He didn't say it out of fear.

He said it out of pride. Out of ego. Out of that same blinding belief that the world bent to his will—and that losing agency was worse than losing life itself.

But when the ambulance came, there was no plug to pull.

The hospital call came after another fall.

It wasn't the first. But this one was different.

This time, the damage was irreversible. The second leg—his last connection to any independence—was beyond saving. The infection had spread; the circulation was gone. They didn't ask for his opinion. They simply said it had to go. Below the knee.

The first leg had been taken nearly a year and a half earlier. That had shaken him.

This—this amputated more than flesh.

It took his fire.

He was transferred to a rehab facility. Not a homecoming. A holding place. A final station in a journey that once sped like a freight train and now crawled like rust.

They tried—physical therapy, mobility sessions, lessons on how to shift weight, transfer chairs, gain balance. But there was nothing left in him that wanted to learn.

He had always been the teacher. The leader. The one who told others how it was going to go.

Now nurses were telling him where to sit, when to eat, when to sleep.

And he hated every second of it.

His 65th birthday came while he was still there.

The family visited. Cake. Smiles. A few decorations taped to the wall. A grandchild sat gently on his lap. Photos were taken.

He would wear a rundown old t-shirt that he was comfortable in, a pair of basketball shorts—clothes chosen not for presentation, but because they were easy. Practical. The armor was gone.

Hanavi didn't say much.

He didn't blow out the candle.

He didn't even look at the camera.

His eyes were fixed—burned into some distant point in the room. Desperation sat behind them. Not sadness. Not pain. Just the quiet shock of a man who had lived like a lion… and now felt like something smaller than the memory of himself.

No speech. No toast. Just a slow exhale, as if part of him had already left.

And while he was in that chair, in that rehab room, the house was falling apart—just like him.

It started with the roof. Heavy rains soaked through the tiles, dripping into buckets and warping ceilings. The leaks had been patched years ago, but water always found its way back.

Then the wiring started to fail. Lights flickered without warning. Whole rooms went dark permanently. Switches stopped responding. It was as if the house had forgotten how to power itself.

The HVAC systems—the lungs and heart of the place—could no longer keep up. They wheezed and clanked, short-cycled, and finally gave out. Some rooms were unbearably hot. Others, freezing.

The walls bled.

Sheetrock collapsed from water rot. Mold festered behind cabinets and corners. The smell was faint but sour—like slow, permanent decay.

This wasn't coincidence. This was symmetry.

The home—like Hanavi—had been built fast, lived in loud, and held together by urgency and instinct. But now, without maintenance, without a plan, without a foundation of protection, both man and home buckled under the weight of time.

He never went back to that house.

But in some way, he already knew.

His body was telling him the same story.

There were no more button-downs. No loose-fitting Tommy Bahama shirts. No jeans or loafers. No jewelry. No wallet. No keys. No image left to maintain.

Just a hospital gown and a lap blanket draped over the place where his legs used to be.

Once, he walked with purpose. Sat in rooms like he owned them. Barked instructions with his chest wide open.

Now, he barely spoke.

Only a man in a chair. Eyes locked on something no one else could see.

A cigar burned down to the very edge, fingers singed and shaking. But he didn't let go.

Because in the end, that cigar wasn't just comfort.

It was control.

It was ritual.

It was rebellion.

The last ember for a man who once lit up every room—

—and now sat waiting, quietly, for the final flicker to fade.

Chapter 14:
The River

It started with a phone call.

Just like it was supposed to.

"There's been a fall," they said.

That was all.

No urgency in the voice. No details that could prepare them. Just the fact that he had been found on the floor, and that paramedics had come.

The message reached his daughter—his emergency contact—not by formal paperwork, but by an unspoken understanding between siblings during the earlier stages of his decline. A precaution. Nothing official. Just a quiet plan for when the unthinkable came knocking.

And now, it had.

They said he was being taken to the hospital. No other details. No sirens in the background. No voices breaking under pressure. Just words—vague, heavy, dangling in the air like a question no one wanted to answer.

But the heart always knows.

By the time he arrived at the hospital, he had already stopped breathing.

They had revived him—barely. His chest no longer rose on its own. Machines had taken over the rhythm of life. A ventilator hissed with every artificial breath, and a monitor recorded the faint remnants of what was left.

But none of that was known to the family yet.

All they were told was: It's not looking good. You should come quickly.

And so they did.

There were no planes boarded. The truth was simpler and heavier than that—plans for the weekend were abandoned, rerouted, anchored in a single destination.

At first, there were no tears. Just silence.

The kind of silence you only hear in hospitals—where time stretches unnaturally, like in the movies, or in the stories of those who have stood in this very place. The light was too white, too unfeeling. The air was too dry. The stillness clung to the skin, pressing in.

The waiting room felt like a tomb.

No one dared to ask, "Is he gone?" because the answer already felt inevitable.

When they were finally brought in, he was already under— his body connected to tubes, surrounded by blinking lights and machines whispering like ghosts. They entered the room in turns. Quiet. Careful. Like they might disturb him if they moved too fast.

He looked peaceful—that's what they told themselves. But the truth was heavier than peace.

The ventilator pumped with an eerie rhythm. A hiss, a pause. A hiss, a pause. A mechanical stand-in for the breath he could no longer take.

The heart monitor kept time—soft beeps that became the only sound anyone found themselves listening for.

They stood there—shoulders brushing, hands twitching, lips trembling.

No one spoke.

What could be said?

He wasn't in pain. But he wasn't there, either. He was somewhere between now and never again.

Then the doctor entered. His face carried the gravity of someone who had said these words before, but never lightly.

"It was a massive brain hemorrhage," he said. "There's no brain activity. The machines are breathing for him now."

Someone asked—because they had to—about surgery. About anything.

"The hemorrhaging is too severe. His pupils are dilated. That means his brain has stopped responding. Even if we operated, it wouldn't matter."

He paused, letting it settle.

"He's already gone."

They heard it.

They didn't want to believe it.

Some froze.

Some shook.

Some collapsed into the nearest arms.

For his eldest, it felt like a river breaking inside—an uncontainable surge rushing through every vein. For others, it came in quiet tremors or fixed stares. The room carried every shade of grief at once: choked sobs, white-knuckled stillness, trembling hands searching for something to hold.

The tears weren't graceful. They were the kind that choke and gut you, carrying years of history, unfinished sentences, and all the should have saids that will never be spoken.

The nurses gave them time.

And then… it was time.

The machines went first, one by one.

The ventilator's last hiss cut short, like a breath ending mid-word.

The monitor slowed.

Once per second.

Then longer.

Then… a flat, merciless line.

And silence—the kind that seeps into the bones and stays there.

This was the moment when all the cards were laid on the table, and the truth was all they could walk away with. And sometimes, you walk away not a winner, not a loser—just with the chance for another day, another fight, another appeal, another deal. But not this time.

In their faith, grief does not get to pause.

Jewish law says the body must be buried before sundown if possible. On Shabbat, the burial waits—but the planning begins instantly.

So even as hearts broke, they moved.

Phone calls to the rabbi. To the funeral home. To relatives abroad. To Israel—just in case.

Questions came like bricks in the dark: Do you want tahara? Who will be the shomer? Can we arrange the chevra kadisha? Do you have a tallit for him?

They hadn't even had an hour with him before the decisions began.

It felt like a betrayal of grief.

It wasn't.

It was duty.

Because in their tradition, honoring the dead means acting with both urgency and reverence. It means carrying the soul to its rest with dignity, even when your own legs barely hold you.

The tahara—the ritual purification—would be performed by the chevra kadisha, the sacred burial society. They would wash his body in silence, reciting prayers, asking forgiveness on his behalf, and dressing him in the simple white garments—tachrichim—that erase status and return every person to the same humility in which they entered the world.

A shomer would keep watch from the moment of death until the burial, reading psalms and sitting near him so that his body was never left alone. It was said the soul hovers nearby until the burial, aware of the presence around it, comforted by the watchfulness.

There would be no open casket, no display. Only a plain wooden casket, free of metal, so the body could return to the earth naturally, as tradition commands. His tallit—a prayer shawl—would be placed over him, one corner cut to signify the end of his earthly duties.

Each choice was deliberate, rooted in centuries of practice, each step a final act of love.

It was not for show.

It was for the soul.

And so, even as the family's grief swelled and fractured, they moved together—through calls, through arrangements, through tears—ensuring that when he left this world, he would be carried out with the dignity and urgency their faith demanded.

And in that movement, they found the first fragile shape of closure.

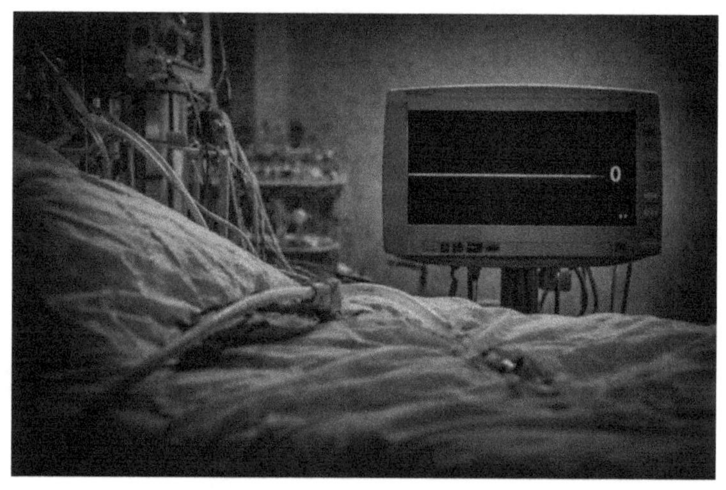

Chapter 15:
The Aftermath

The burial came fast.

In Jewish law, the body must return to the earth before sundown—or as soon as possible, unless it's Shabbat. There was no time for long deliberation. No space to collapse beneath the weight of sorrow. Just a narrow window to act— to honor, to arrange, to release.

In the fog of exhaustion and shock, it was the younger daughter and her husband who stepped up. Without hesitation. Without question. Like two steady hands guided by something higher. While the rest of the family stood suspended in surreal grief, they moved. Phone calls. Logistics. Coordination. It all came together with a grace that felt almost preordained. They made sure Hanavi would be laid to rest with dignity.

The chevra kadisha—the sacred burial society—was present. The tahara was performed, washing his body with reverence and prayer. A shomer sat beside him, reading psalms through the night. The rabbi who knew him best agreed to lead the service. There was something holy in that, too. Like the world had conspired to make this farewell right, even if nothing about it felt real.

When the moment came, they stood by as the man who once filled every room with his voice, his motion, his smoke, and his command… was lowered into the earth under ancient prayers and a sky too still for words.

Most of us haven't really been to many funerals. We don't know what to expect. Some picture wailing. Others imagine long speeches or polished eulogies. What we found was quieter—less scripted. His sisters flew in from Israel. To them, it was shattering. For some, grief was loud. For others, it lived in silence. And for a few, like his eldest son, the sorrow stayed tucked behind the eyes, lodged deep in the throat.

Faces in the crowd stood out—some expected, some surprising, and others noticeably absent. But in that moment, only one thing truly mattered: the people who were there. That was enough.

And then, as tradition dictates, the focus shifted from loss to action. From ceremony to ritual. From death… to duty.

They ripped their garments—keriah—a symbolic tear across the heart. And they returned home.

But home… wasn't home anymore.

The Israeli network wasn't playing on the television. His chair was empty. The air hung heavier. The house wasn't just quiet—it was hollow. Like something had been scooped out of its center and taken with him.

Shiva began. For seven days, they sat. People came. They brought food, prayers, stories. Some moments were warm. Others were blurred by exhaustion. The cycle was dizzying—open doors, full trays, sympathetic eyes. Beneath it all was the undeniable truth: the house no longer had a pulse. He was no longer at the center. The gravity had gone.

In quieter moments, they remembered. They thought of the way he once sat shiva for his own father, nearly twenty-seven years earlier. They thought about how fast it all goes—from one graveside to the next.

The shiva passed in a haze. Some came to mourn. Others came with veiled intentions. A few realtors stopped by, offering condolences that quickly bled into, "Let me know when you're ready to talk about the house."

It felt hollow—like grief was just another transaction waiting for its turn.

The ones who came to remember—truly remember—are the ones that mattered. But grief doesn't end with burial. It lingers. It drips. It waits in quiet corners and memory fragments. Sometimes it arrives in the scent of his cologne still clinging to a jacket. Sometimes it's the buzz of a phone he'll never answer. Sometimes it's silence so loud it's deafening.

And always, it carries the question: Did we listen enough? Did we stay long enough? Did we say what needed to be said before time ran out?

The lesson he left wasn't something he spoke—it was something he lived: never be afraid to go after what you want. He didn't wait for permission. He forged paths where none existed. He lived boldly—sometimes questionably, but always decisively.

Maybe the world he thrived in doesn't exist anymore. But relentlessness? Fortitude with an edge? The nerve to do what others won't? Those still hold weight.

Yet the world itself has changed. Where once stories lingered in half-truths and word-of-mouth, everything now moves faster. Fact-checking is instantaneous. News spreads in seconds. And now, with the arrival of artificial intelligence and all it has proven to do in its infant stages, we've stepped into a new terrain—one where memory, truth, and even legacy can be tested, recorded, and preserved in ways our fathers never imagined.

Chapter 16:
Settling the Chips

When shiva ended, the house changed.

The trays were emptied, chairs stacked, the stream of visitors thinned to nothing. What replaced the noise was not peace, but a silence that carried unfinished business. The kind that stood in the doorway and asked: Now what?

No one in the family lived there anymore, but the house—his house—still stood. Barely. A weary frame with a leaking roof that turned rainstorms into indoor waterfalls. There was no system to catch the water, no bucket big enough to keep pace. The electricity stuttered. The water bills had been rising for months. Each problem was fixable, but none had been prepared for. No emergency fund. No cushion hidden away.

Insurance existed, but it had been taken too late, and the claims went nowhere. Not because there hadn't been an effort—but because the effort came after the window had already closed.

Now the burden was tangible. Structural. Heavy.

Someone had to step in. The eldest son did. Not because anyone asked, but because silence leaves no volunteers—only those who feel the pull. He waded into probate first, the initial battlefield. The house was already tangled in litigation. Auction notices were circling. Creditors were lining up.

It was homesteaded—that was the thin shield. Enough to buy a little time.

He used that time well. Paperwork bought weeks. Signatures bought months. Through that narrow gap, an opportunity slipped in: an interested buyer. The deal closed just before the walls closed in. The sale turned what was almost a total loss into a modest cushion—enough for his mother to have a fragment of peace. A sliver of dignity. Something resembling a retirement.

Because truthfully, Hanavi had left her nothing.

No deed in her name.

No life insurance.

No steady income.

No instructions.

Only a collapsing home—and six children.

She carried the grief heavily, but it was layered with devotion. She had loved him loudly, painfully, faithfully. He had given her a family, a lifetime of motion, and the noise of a man who refused to be small. But when that roar stopped, the quiet left a void no one could fill.

They each carried pieces of him. But no one knew where all the pieces were.

There had been other possessions once—valuable ones. The gold Daytona Rolex had vanished years earlier. The son didn't know if it had been pawned or lost. His mother gave him Hanavi's cigar lighter instead. He still kept it, feeling its weight often. In his home, he hung a photo of Hanavi receiving a blessing from a rabbi, the elder's hand firm on his head—a moment that captured both his father's fire and his fragility.

The house itself was only a hollow shell now. It had once overflowed—crowded hallways, voices shouting over the television, the smell of coffee and cigars drifting through every doorway. Those years lived like a snapshot from a time that no longer existed—an era of unfiltered arguments, doorsteps crowded with shoes, and nights thick with ritual. A time now found only on old screens and in the pages of memoirs.

Sometimes, the son still waited for the phone to ring—Hanavi asking him to come fix the WiFi or the Israeli channel, impatient that he couldn't find it himself. But the call didn't come. It never would again.

There had been no single breaking point. Just an accumulation of truths that weighed heavier with time.

Each sibling had their own lens, their own story. The man they remembered was not always kind. He could be loud, dismissive, self-serving. But he also had traits that could not be replicated—a door open to strangers, a courage without ceiling, a belief in motion so fierce it felt like survival. He gave love the only way he knew—without brakes or balance.

But he rarely stopped to ask how it felt to receive it.

Hanavi had been a man born of survival, shaped by a period when endurance was the only language worth speaking, and permanence was something you built with your hands.

And now, they were left to sort not just his absence, but the aftermath of his choices—carrying him forward in objects, flashbacks, and echoes. Trying to stitch together a legacy from what had been left unsaid.

In the quiet after his passing, the house felt less like a home and more like the last uncashed chip from a long, high-stakes game—a chip he had never redeemed, a hand he had never shown. The table was empty now, the cards already folded, but the bet remained on the felt, waiting for someone else to decide what it was worth.

And in that stillness, the truth was impossible to ignore:

He had played for the moment, believing there would always be another deal, another chance, another turn.

But time is the one opponent you cannot outplay.

And when the final hand is called, what's left behind is not the pile you built, but what survives after you've left the table.

Epilogue:
The Bet That Outlived the Player

There is no grand prize at the end of a life like my father's.

No ticker-tape parade. No gold-plated legacy. No ceremony handing over a clean slate to the next generation.

There is only what remains.

A house once full of motion and smoke, now hollow.

A family bound by love, but carrying unanswered questions.

Paperwork. Probate. A cigar lighter passed from father to son.

A story — raw, incomplete, filled with fire and silence.

For all his flaws, my father lived louder than most men dream. He didn't follow rules because he knew rules were written against men like him. So he made his own. And when they failed, he pivoted. Again and again, until his body could no longer keep pace with the bets he was placing.

But the truth is, he was never really betting on money.

He was betting on time.

Time to recover.

Time to win.

Time to provide.

Time to say the things he never said.

Time to build the foundation he never built.

But time is the one opponent none of us can bluff. And in the end, the final bet wasn't at the poker table. It was the assumption that later would come. But later never came.

When it was over, the images that stayed weren't just memories. They were photographs: him on his yacht, captain's hat tilted, cigar glowing against the Miami sky. Him young and flexing in front of friends, muscles tight, laughter rolling. Him bowed beneath the hands of a rabbi, eyes shut as blessing pressed down like gravity.

And then there are the objects. My mother handing me his lighter — not as a torch to keep smoking in his name, but as something to hold when the silence feels too heavy.

That silence has been the hardest part.

The phone that once rang four, five times a day no longer rings at all. His voice — urgent, demanding, impossible to ignore — is gone. Those interruptions used to drive me crazy. But now, I'd give anything for one more flick-of-the-finger request. Because life itself disappears like that — like a flame blown out, leaving only the smoke.

Yet even in the silence, I've learned something. Time ran out for him. But not for me. Not for my children. That's why this story exists — so they can understand his fire, but also his flaws. His flaws weren't rooted in malice. They were human. He always fell forward. But because he never built the foundation to catch himself, every fall became another scramble, another gamble, another survival.

My father's gift was his ability to bend chaos into control, to make the unsteady feel certain. That made him magnetic. But it also meant he never left the storm.

So now, at forty-five, I carry his story differently. I choose to learn from it, to act on it. To build the structure he never did, so my children won't inherit silence. Because the greatest inheritance isn't motion. It's meaning.

That is the bet I refuse to gamble with.

If my father taught me anything, it's that motion alone can take you far — but not forever. To play only for today is to gamble tomorrow away.

So learn. Act. Build. Protect. Teach your children. Write it down. Fund it. Share it.

Because in the end, the greatest bet you'll ever place is not at the table. It's at the foundation of your family.

And the only way to win… is to prepare.

Part II

Reflection on
The Gambler's Mind

When I think about my father, Hanavi, I don't just see the man everyone else saw — loud, confident, decisive. I see the boy he once was, growing up in a brand-new Israel, where the air was thick with survival and pride, and where every move mattered because the country itself was still learning how to stand.

I picture him on that moped, a young soldier on base, running out of gas and "borrowing" fuel because in his mind, waiting for permission was a foreign concept. He got caught, of course, and spent time locked up. Even if it was brief, it left a scar — not the kind you see on the skin, but the kind that rewires the way a man thinks. From that day on, he swore no one would ever again have the power to trap him.

That vow became his oxygen. For my father, stillness felt like suffocating. And maybe that's why he thrived in motion — flipping deals, chasing opportunities, gambling when others hesitated.

But here's what I didn't understand back then — and what I want you to hear now: motion is not the same as progress. You can be moving all the time and still be going in circles. My father's speed was unmatched, but speed without a map can take you further from where you need to be.

Motion alone doesn't mean anything. It reminds me of a joke from work: if you walk quickly with purpose, as if you're on a mission, most people won't stop you. They'll assume you're headed somewhere important. In reality, you might just be going from point A to point B without wanting to get interrupted. That's motion — not progress. It looks intentional, but it's empty without direction.

I grew up thinking this was the model for success: act fast, trust your gut, never let anyone see you pause. And there's truth in that — decisiveness is a weapon. You can't sit around overthinking while the deal passes you by. In our tradition, there's an old saying that the wise person sees what is being born — not just what is in front of them. My father saw the birth of opportunity before others noticed. The problem was, he didn't always see what those opportunities would grow into years later.

And me? I was blind to it. Comfort coddled me. I did what was required, never more. I didn't ask questions about trusts or wills or compounding wealth. Why would I? My father was handling things. I thought motion meant safety. But safety without structure is an illusion.

It wasn't until much later — after I'd read books like What Would the Rockefellers Do, The Jewish Phenomenon, Rich Dad Poor Dad, Think and Grow Rich — that I realized the wealthiest families don't just work hard. They build systems. They set rules for their money the way our faith sets rules for our lives. They pass down not just assets, but instructions. And here's the kicker: if you don't know the rules of the game, you're just another chip on someone else's table.

That's the irony: my father could walk into a card room and read a table in seconds, but we never sat at our own kitchen table to talk about reading a balance sheet, creating a trust, or insulating assets. We never discussed how to make money stay.

And that's what I need you to see — decisiveness is nothing without direction. My father's gift was his ability to act in the moment. That's power. But without the wisdom to aim that power — without a plan to protect it — you're just burning fuel until the tank runs dry.

So here's my challenge to you: don't just move. Learn. Invest in yourself first — because knowledge is power, but only if you pair it with the courage to act. Our faith teaches that you protect what you build, the same way you build a fence around your vineyard. My father taught me the action part. Life taught me the protection part.

You need both. If you're only learning but never moving, you're stuck. If you're only moving but never learning, you're lost.

I've lived both. Trust me balance is the only game worth playing.

Reflection on
The Cost of Winning

I must have been six or seven when I asked my father for those Rocky gloves. To me, they weren't about boxing. They were about connection. I wanted something that said, Even when you're far away, I'm still in your thoughts.

He was in America then, hustling alone while we stayed behind in Israel. I asked over the phone, and he laughed that warm laugh of his and said, "I'll bring them." When you're a kid, you believe promises like that. You don't hear the weight in a father's voice, or the stress beneath his breath. You just hear yes.

I also remember the first time I tasted home fries. We were fresh off the plane in Philadelphia, living in the Roosevelt Inn. A plate came out with a thick omelet and crispy diced potatoes fried golden brown. It was simple food, but to me, it was proof that a whole new world had opened.

Not long after, we moved into a small brick rowhome. No backyard, creaky floors, kids packed into bedrooms — but it was ours. Our neighbor's son was a little older than me, and his father was Joe Frazier. That Joe Frazier. The heavyweight champion of the world. He'd pull up, and the whole block would shift. People nodded. Kids froze mid-play. Neighbors peered through blinds. Greatness had parked right next door.

That's how I saw my father back then, too — larger than life. I remember one trip in Israel, before we ever left, maybe up north to Mount Hermon. We stopped somewhere to eat, and I sat with my mother, watching him at another table surrounded by friends and cousins. They were laughing, flexing in some mock contest, and when he went last, I swore he won. I didn't care if it was a joke — in my eyes, he had just beaten everyone in the room. That was who my father was to me. Untouchable.

But even then, beneath the laughter, he was always in motion. Fixing cars. Driving cabs. Sitting at poker tables in smoky backrooms. I didn't see it then, but he wasn't playing for the thrill. He was playing not to lose.

When the wins came, they stretched just far enough. Rent. Tuition. Groceries. Gas. For him, winning often meant nothing more than keeping the family afloat without asking anyone for help.

It took me decades to understand what that meant. Some people think winning is about more — more money, more toys, more "yes" moments. But for men like him, winning was about avoiding collapse.

The problem is when you're always playing defense, you rarely get to go on offense. You don't think about trusts, compound interest, family banks, or how dynasties preserve wealth. You think about next week's bills.

And here's where my own ignorance came in. Comfort shielded me from the urgency he lived with. I didn't see the unopened envelopes, the quiet arguments, the sacrifices behind the hospitality. I wasn't asking about wills or structures. Why would I? He was handling it.

But I've since learned something that changes everything: the wealthy aren't lucky. They're prepared. They use moments of stability to build insulation. They expect the winter even in the summer. They know the car will break, the market will dip, the storm will come. And they plan for it.

In our tradition, we're told to fill the storehouse before famine, to prepare in summer for what we'll need in winter. That's not just agriculture. That's life.

If I could speak to that little boy asking for Rocky gloves, I'd tell him:

Yes, dream. Yes, believe. But also learn the rules of the game. Don't just watch greatness walk down the block — ask what made it last after the lights went out.

Because motion is survival. But structure is freedom.

My father mastered motion.

I had to teach myself structure.

And if you're reading this, you have the chance to learn both before life forces it on you.

Don't just play not to lose. Play to win — and to keep winning.

Reflection on
The Ante

Walking into the Northeast Philadelphia house for the first time was like stepping onto a movie set. We were still in shock from leaving Israel, still adjusting to the idea that this — America — was now home. I'd seen American houses in films, but it's different when you're inside one, and it's supposed to be yours. Carpet underfoot, instead of hard tile. The kitchen with its old linoleum squares that seemed to hold decades of footsteps.

The backyard wasn't endless, but for us it was space enough to run, enough to imagine. And then there was the basement. I don't remember ever having a basement in Israel. There, some homes had a lower level because of the slope of the land. But this was different. You went down, and it was a whole other world under the house.

At first, it felt cinematic. Eventually, like anything, you get used to it. But I still remember that first impression — the way the light hit the red brick outside, the way the air inside felt cooler than expected, the way my father stood in the doorway like he was claiming more than just a house.

Life inside those walls fell quickly into rhythm. Shabbat every Friday night, no matter how the week had gone. White tablecloth. Candles. Wine. My mother's cooking — sometimes stretched thinner than it should have been, but it always worked out. Guests were constant. At that age, it didn't bother me. It was just life. Later, in Cherry Hill and Miami, I'd start to notice the cost of that open door, and I knew my mother sometimes wished it was just us. But back then, I didn't think about it.

The garage was my father's second home, though in those days I wasn't working alongside him yet. It wasn't until my early teens that I'd start spending real time there. Even so, I remember the characters that moved through it.

Larry — a fellow cabbie — impossible to forget. Blonde hair, wiry build, a way of speaking that felt just left of center. He'd stick out his hand and say, "Hi, I am Larry," in this odd, almost practiced tone. I couldn't tell if it was an accent or just his own rhythm, but to me, still new to English, it sounded like its own language.

Then there was the Guyanese man, another cab driver who became close to my father — the kind of friend who shows up so often they feel like family furniture. In the beginning, they were thick as thieves. Later, life and purpose pulled them apart. But for a time, he was a fixture in my father's orbit.

And then there was that phrase: still in the game. I can't remember the first time I heard him say it. It never came with ceremony. Just a quiet proclamation after a long day, shoes off, legs stretched, my mother kneeling without complaint to help him unwind. Still in the game meant the hand wasn't over, the cards weren't folded, there was still another move to make. At the time, I didn't think much of it. But it was the sound of resilience, a declaration that tomorrow wasn't lost.

And my mother — God bless her — she was the most selfless partner I've ever seen. Raising six kids, supporting him in every way possible. Whether she wanted that life or not, she bore it. Always. Loyalty like that is its own kind of strength. You don't see the full weight of it as a kid — you just live inside the results of it.

My father never explained his vision back then. He wasn't a man of explanations. That came later, in Cherry Hill, when he started talking about legacy: This is all for you. But in those early Northeast Philly years, it was simpler. It wasn't legacy yet. It was about planting roots and proving we could stand.

Looking back, I realize this was the chapter where I first learned the feeling of "arriving," even if we weren't there yet. A moment when survival started to look like stability. And maybe that's why he whispered still in the game — because for him, the game wasn't just about money or business. It was about being able to look around, even for one quiet moment, and know he was still standing.

Reflection on Raising the Stakes

I can still see that drive into Cherry Hill. Crossing the bridge felt like leaving one world and entering another. Whether it was the Ben Franklin or one of the others, I can't remember — but I remember the feeling. You pass the tolls, the city drops behind you, and suddenly you're in a place where the streets curve wide, the air feels quieter, and the houses stand back from the road like they have nothing to prove.

Then we turned into our new neighborhood. Big houses lined the street, each one planted with intention. We drove all the way to the end of the cul-de-sac, and there it was — tall, white, four columns rising in the front. To me it looked like a postcard, a suburban version of the White House. For a kid who had grown up in Israel and then in the rowhomes of Northeast Philly, it felt like a leap across worlds. I remember telling people, almost bragging, "It's a quarter-million-dollar house," which in 1995 sounded enormous.

The lot was nearly an acre, with wooded areas behind it, a Florida room that flooded with light, and a kitchen where my mom always seemed to have someone helping her keep things in order. My own space ended up in the basement. With six kids in the house, it was the only way to carve out room to breathe. Down there, I had my own corner of the world, away from the constant motion upstairs.

But before Cherry Hill, there was the other project — the second house my father built right next to our place in Northeast Philly. I was there through every stage of construction. I'd walk through its skeleton while it was going up, stepping over planks, peeking through open frames, imagining what it would be like when it was finished. For a while, I even lived in one of its bedrooms before he rented it out. It felt like a step up — proof he was moving forward.

And then there was the day the FBI came. You can't forget something like that. One second, the house was quiet. The next, agents were everywhere — over fences, through doors, across the yard. Windbreakers flashing, moving fast. No matter where you looked, someone was closing in. I froze, hands up, not knowing what was happening. My mother was in another room, just as confused. It ended as suddenly as it began. They didn't cuff him in front of me; I never saw that part. But afterward, the detectives sat us down and asked questions: How did we know him? What was he like? How had he ended up in our home? Then they were gone. That was the last time I ever saw him or his daughter.

Around that same time, my grandfather — my father's father — was nearing the end of his life back in Israel. I had only met him once more at my Bar Mitzvah. At thirteen, it was strange to meet someone you knew was family but didn't actually know. When word came that he had passed, it wasn't a shock. We knew he had been sick. My father knew it was coming, too. But knowing doesn't make the weight lighter when the call finally comes.

I think his death shifted something in my father. He wasn't religious in the traditional sense — he never kept strict observance — but he held reverence for tradition. And in that period, he started leaning toward Kabbalah. Maybe it was faith. Maybe it was desperation. Maybe it was just the search for leverage, another way to bend the world to his will. What I know is this: he was looking for permanence.

Looking back, I see it clearer. Permanence doesn't come from bigger houses or spiritual shortcuts. It comes from planning. From building something that doesn't collapse when you do. From systems that can carry a family forward.

Cherry Hill wasn't just another move. It was a statement: We've made it here.

But for me, the lesson was different: expansion without protection is fragile. And permanence without planning is only an illusion.

Reflection on
Leveraged Hands

I was standing right next to him when it happened.

It started as nothing — just a man unlocking his own office. He slid the key in, gave it a jiggle, and when it didn't turn, he tried again. A little more pressure. A little more impatience. Then that moment where you know — it's not the wrong key. It's the right key, but the lock has been changed.

The office doors were glass, and through them you could see enough to know things weren't right. The furniture wasn't in place. Papers gone. The hum of life that used to buzz behind those doors — silenced.

I asked him, naïve as I was at the time, "Did you guys move offices or something? Did you forget to tell me?" Maybe they'd relocated, maybe there was a rent issue, maybe there was some logical reason. I didn't realize I was adding to the storm already building in his chest.

But he knew. His eyes weren't searching for answers — they were confirming what he already suspected. He picked up the phone, called the one person he needed to, and when the voice on the other end answered, he let loose. I'd never heard him like that. It wasn't yelling in the way people think of yelling — it was louder than loud. It started sharp, then dropped lower, until the words collapsed into nothing but breath, like the rage had burned the air right out of him.

After that, it's a blur. I think we went to someone else's office, maybe an attorney, maybe another partner, maybe an apartment we kept downtown so we didn't have to get a hotel. But that front door — that sound of a key failing in a familiar lock — stayed with me.

Before that day, that office was its own ecosystem. Leather chairs, wood desks, people at the front desk forwarding calls, others keeping the books, others hunting the next deal. My father was at the center, everything flowing through his direction. Some partners looked like professionals you could trust in any room. Others… well, now I can see they were just riding along, waiting for a chance to take what they could.

I was working with him then — learning the business, running payroll, handling construction sites, doing the banking, taking on whatever task was needed. I was in it, not just watching. And then, in a single moment, the office was gone. I never stepped foot inside again.

The court battles dragged on for years, until every asset tied to it was liquidated. And in that time, I heard a lot about betrayal, about trust, about how people change. The truth is, going into business with someone requires trust — but it also needs protection.

It's like asking the love of your life for a prenup. They'll say, "If you trust me, why do we need it?" The answer is simple: because trust alone is not a plan.

If you love, respect, and value something enough — whether it's a marriage, a friendship, or a business — you protect it by every means available. Not because you expect it to fail, but because you know people change, circumstances shift, and life doesn't always give you time to prepare.

Agreements aren't just for the two people signing them. They protect everyone who might one day be affected — families, employees, partners you haven't even met yet.

That's the lesson I carried from that glass door: love and loyalty are powerful, but they aren't armor. Protection is.

Reflection on
Breaking Point

Miami in those days felt like the pinnacle. Sunshine almost every day. New cars in the driveway. New toys arriving like clockwork. Jet skis tied up by the dock. The yacht sitting there like a promise. For me, daily life was easy — I didn't feel the pressure my father carried. We were living in paradise, and the horizon felt endless.

The house itself was its own statement. In the living room, a teal leather sectional wrapped around the space like something from a magazine spread. Two rotating recliners flanked the corners. The 42-inch television sat neatly in the middle of a built-in entertainment wall unit — the kind of setup you noticed the second you walked in. This wasn't Cherry Hill anymore. This was Miami. This was the ultimate upgrade.

The morning of September 11th, 2001, started like any other. My mother was in the kitchen, moving through her routine with quiet focus. I woke up late, wandered into the living room, the smell of breakfast drifting in from the other room. I glanced at the screen — and for a moment, I thought I was catching the start of a movie.

It took my mother's voice from the kitchen to break the illusion: "It's not a movie. It's real."

The air in the room shifted instantly. I sank into the couch, watching the chaos unfold. The teal leather felt cold against my arms. The sound from the TV filled the space, drowning everything else. I don't remember speaking much — just watching, taking it in, feeling something I couldn't name.

My father wasn't home that morning. He was out in motion, in his prime, chasing deals. He had a gift for locking things under contract before anyone else could. At that stage, I never saw any sign of financial struggle. The only thing I ever heard him mention was money being tied up longer than expected. But somehow, he always maneuvered around it.

What I didn't understand then was that with each upgrade in status, the size of the debts upgraded too. Bigger house, bigger toys, bigger risks. That was the pattern. And while we were living in the sunlight, the shadows were already stretching longer.

Looking back, I realize that morning in September was a pivot — not just for the country, but for us. For me, it's frozen in memory: my mother in the kitchen, the teal couch, the recliners, the television glowing from the wall unit, and a world — our world — that seemed secure in the moment but was already shifting beneath our feet.

Reflection on
Let It Ride

When the Bell's Palsy hit, none of us knew what it meant. Would it be permanent? Would it get worse? Those were the questions in the back of my mind. His speech was a little slurred, half his face refusing to move the way it used to — but if you didn't know him well, you might not even notice. He didn't slow down his talking, his negotiating, or his schedule. And he certainly didn't let it change how he carried himself. He pushed through it, like everything else, and got past it faster than I expected.

That period was a blur of planes, phone calls, and shifting time zones. I was with him on those flights between Miami and Syracuse, in and out of upstate New York, where we were working deals with a whole new set of partners. That came with its own chaos — everyone wanting to do things their way, but my father's formula never changed: You bring the money for the acquisition, we do the work. It was simple, and it worked, as long as everyone played their part.

Then there was Oklahoma. The property after Hurricane Katrina. He was proud of that one — not just because it was a deal, but because it felt like a good deed. Housing evacuees at reduced rent gave him a sense of doing something bigger than himself. Maybe there were conversations behind closed doors, maybe he thought it might return some favor down the road. I don't know. What I do know is that, at the time, it felt genuine. You could see it in the way he talked about it.

Back in Miami, he was always in "full presence" mode. The house and the backyard were the hub. The yacht wasn't just for leisure — it was a stage. Guests came through constantly. Deals were discussed over drinks, over meals, against the hum of water against the hull. Evenings could start with laughter at dinner and end with the quiet satisfaction of business moved forward without ever setting foot in an office.

I was still living at home then, working with him every day. There was no sense of an ending. We just kept moving — winging it, riding momentum. Even when friction showed up, even when the cracks were visible in deals and relationships, it never felt like we were running out of road.

Looking back, I can see how easy it is to mistake motion for permanence. We were so sure the game would go on forever that we didn't stop to think about what it would mean if the cards ran out.

Reflection on
All-In, No Exit

When I first heard about Vista Del Cielo, it wasn't like my father was pitching just another building. This was his play for the skyline. I had seen him watch partners pull off their own verticals in Miami, seen the pride it gave them. This was going to be his version of that — whether it was fully his or in partnership didn't matter. In his mind, this was the tower that would carry his name in spirit.

The sales trailer was something else. I remember stepping inside and feeling like every detail was built to impress — polished counters, glossy renderings, the scent of fresh coffee and expensive cologne in the air. A realtor was on-site, ready to walk prospects through the dream. A banker sat nearby, prepared to take pre-sale deposits on the spot. It had the energy of a deal already in motion, the kind of environment where you could almost believe the building was already on the skyline and not just on paper.

At home, there was no tension. Business felt smooth. The younger kids weren't under any pressure — they were in their own worlds. I was proud of what he was doing. We all were.

Then came the call. I was right there when he took it. His voice carried a tremor I didn't hear often. When he hung up, he said flatly, "He pulled out."

I asked, "Pulled out of what?" and that's when he told me — the lead investor, the partner who was going to take this project across the starting line, was gone.

He was concerned, but he didn't stop. The survival instinct took over. Phone calls went out. Names were checked. What he didn't have his ear to was the deeper tremor in the market itself. This was late 2007, heading into 2008. He didn't believe in following market news, but the financial ground was already shifting. Banks were slicing up mortgages into securities, packaging and selling them like stock, moving paper faster than bricks could be laid. When the bottom fell out, those paper assets collapsed in value, and credit lines dried up almost overnight.

I was there when he signed the bridge loan. We were all in the office. If there was worry in him, he didn't let it surface. His energy was conviction — as if he'd just struck gold and the only thing left was to mine it. To him, signing wasn't a risk; it was the final green light.

When Del Cielo went down, it wasn't because he hadn't put in the work or the belief. It was timing — brutal, uncooperative timing. You can prepare for almost anything in business, but you can't make time bend for you. And if you're not prepared for time's turns, it can gut you in an instant.

What I remember most about that period isn't the loss of the yacht or the cars or the Phantom. It's how quickly he shifted from disappointment back into motion. He might have been emotional, might have reacted in ways that weren't conventional, but he didn't retreat. For him, even after an all-in bet that didn't land, the only move was forward. Always forward.

Reflection on
Down to the Felt

I never saw that penthouse office before it was finished. By the time I walked in, it already looked like every space he had ever claimed as his own — remodeled the moment he got the keys. Fresh flooring, new furniture, everything polished to say: this is where deals happen. It was his standard playbook. Take a blank space, dress it for opportunity, and make it feel alive.

I wasn't part of the setup this time. My focus was elsewhere. I had a family to support, and I needed steady income, not bursts or trickles. That meant my days were spent where the paychecks were predictable. I didn't have the luxury — or the appetite — for the swings that came with chasing new ventures from scratch.

Still, I saw the flow through that office. People came in with equity offers or with keys to spaces they wanted someone else to take over. One of those was a restaurant at the Hard Rock. The lease required an Asian fusion concept, so that's what we created. From day one, it was a challenge — high-cost, high-maintenance, demanding constant capital just to keep the doors open.

The office was busy, but not in the way his earlier spaces had been. It wasn't a full-scale command center buzzing with deals and phone calls. It was more like a staging ground — a place to catch whatever opportunity walked in and see if it could be turned into cash.

I saw it less as strategy and more as habit. This was the foundation he knew: lease the space, make it look the part, use it as a magnet for deals. It was the environment where his kind of success had always been manufactured.

But for me, it was a reminder that familiarity and sustainability aren't the same thing. Just because something looks alive doesn't mean it's built to last.

Reflection on Drawing Dead

His office was always his fortress. Even in this period, when the business itself had thinned down to shadows, he still took the back office — the biggest one, with the heavy antique-styled furniture in deep reds and browns. Against one wall sat a cabinet where he kept his collection of die-cast steel replica cars, as if they were trophies of roads traveled and races won. A flat screen hung high, always tuned to the Israeli network. That way he could keep a finger on the pulse of what was happening back home and never miss a match when Beitar Yerushalayim was playing.

Walking into his office felt familiar. Authoritative. Curated. Distinctly his. Even when there was little business left to conduct, the space still carried the air of command.

Downstairs, the building itself was a mix of professionals and small shops. A pharmacy. An eye doctor. A Cuban restaurant. And tucked among them, a little bodega. It wasn't much different from a gas station convenience store — lottery tickets at the counter, shelves of snacks, the faint smell of smoke products. For him, that bodega became ritual. Almost daily, he'd walk down, grab a chocolate, and buy a lottery ticket.

It wasn't about the odds. It was about the hope. A quiet prayer wrapped in foil and numbers. Maybe today would be the day it all turned around.

He kept that office suite long after there was real business to be done there. It wasn't about utility. It was about identity.

Leasing out parts of the space gave the illusion of motion, maybe even a trickle of cash flow, but the office itself was his anchor. The last bluff. The last place where he could still sit behind a desk and feel like he was in the game.

When he knew money was coming in — a small deal closing, a rental check clearing, a promise of funds — he'd take to a notebook or even loose sheets of paper. He'd start budgeting, prioritizing, writing out who needed to be paid first, how the debt could be cleared, what order made the most sense. He strategized constantly on paper. But rarely did those lists make it past the ink. There was always a variable that shifted, always a factor that knocked the plan off course. Maybe for him, the writing itself was enough. Maybe seeing it on paper was the comfort.

Physically, the only real change was age. Not old, but older. We urged him to walk more, to move, to care for himself in ways he never wanted to. But he was set in his ways. Motion and fluidity were his lifeblood. To create rigid plans for the future, to put instructions on paper about what would happen after him — maybe to him, that felt like surrender. Maybe it felt like admitting the game was over.

That's probably why we never pressed harder about planning. By then, the truth was, there wasn't much left to plan. Some options could have been put on the table — there always are — but for him, options meant constraint. And constraint meant the end of fluid motion.

For my father, even in those quiet rituals of chocolate and lottery tickets, it was never about the result. It was about rhythm. About keeping the illusion alive — that there was still another move to be made.

Reflection on
The Illusion of Control

I don't remember exactly where I was when the second stroke happened — most likely at work — but I remember being home when he returned with my mother. That's when it began.

At first, it felt like an argument, the kind I'd known all my life. He accused, I defended. That was the rhythm with him — if he pointed, you were guilty until proven otherwise. But this was different. He wasn't arguing for the sake of being right. He was looking around the house we had lived in for decades and swearing it wasn't his.

He said the door was different. That we had replaced it. That we'd sold his house out from under him and rebuilt a copy. His eyes scanned every detail like they were pieces of evidence. It was as if he was living in a nightmare — his greatest fear — that control had slipped away, that his agency had been stolen.

Everyone else stayed quiet, but I was already in the middle of it, trying to reason with him, trying to calm him down, trying to fight the urge to defend myself. And yet, nothing I said mattered. With him, getting into an argument always meant you were wrong, even when you weren't. But now it wasn't just stubbornness. It was real. He was seeing something that wasn't there, and he believed it completely.

It was scary. It was frustrating. How do you fight with a vision that only exists in someone else's mind?

I called a mutual attorney we knew, desperate for clarity — not for control, but for understanding. All I got was a vague suggestion about power of attorney. Nothing concrete. No direction. No one sat us down to say: here's what you need, here's who you should call, here's how to protect him — and yourselves. We were on our own, staring at the gap between what should have been prepared and the silence we inherited instead.

It wasn't just the house. There were nights he would take the car out at odd hours. Once, I tracked him through his SIM ID and found him at the Hard Rock Casino in the middle of the night. He was still on heavy medication, and later I learned that recovery from a stroke can take hours, sometimes days, for the mind to clear. That didn't make it less terrifying to realize how fragile everything had become.

That period was a warning — a heavy toll that made us hope full incapacitation would never come. And yet, instead of forcing the hard conversations, we slipped back into routine once he seemed more himself. We told ourselves he was safe in his realm again. We stayed close enough to keep a pulse, but not close enough to confront what it really meant.

Because confronting it would have meant admitting what none of us wanted to: that the man who had always insisted on control was no longer in control at all.

Reflection on
Dead Man's Hand

I wasn't at the hospital for the amputations. None of us children were. Only my mother. She carried that weight alone — sitting through the surgeries, hearing the updates in real time, being the one who had to sign when signatures were needed. We all had families of our own, responsibilities we couldn't step away from. And in some ways, maybe we just didn't have the strength to stand in those rooms.

At some point, we all knew about the DNR. It wasn't a surprise. My father had said it for years — he didn't want to live crippled, didn't want to go on as a handicap. Signing that document was consistent with the way he lived: direct, defiant, unwilling to surrender agency to anyone else. Intellectually, it made sense. Emotionally, it was devastating. Knowing the paper was there, knowing what it meant, was crippling in its own way. None of us wanted to face what it foreshadowed. So, in our own ways, we brushed it aside and kept going, pretending there was more time.

My mother didn't have that luxury. She became the full-time caregiver — the role no one asks for, but the one she bore without choice. We helped where it was convenient: adjusting him in his chair, pushing the wheelchair, keeping him comfortable. But she was the one doing the real work. She was the one behind the scenes — lifting him in and out of the shower, dressing and undressing him, feeding him, sitting with him as he poured out frustration and grief. She became his therapist, his nurse, his anchor — on top of being his wife.

I believe depression set in during those later years. The silence weighed heavy. For a man who had once filled rooms with his presence, the absence of movement was unbearable. He leaned on medication. He used to tell me he needed to "shut his brain off." And I understood that more than I wanted to. It's the same reason I fall asleep with the TV on — the noise helps you escape your own mind. Silence drags you back into every worry, every regret.

For most people, you can tell yourself it's God's plan, that if you do your best, the result will be as it should. But for lions like my father, that wasn't enough. He couldn't settle into faith alone. His way of coping was to medicate, to numb. And while I saw my sisters' point of view — that it only made things worse — I also understood it. For him, those pills, that escape, brought a little comfort in a world where comfort had been stripped away.

I can't imagine the toll he carried — physically, mentally. I hope I never have to. What I do know is that for a man who once lived by instinct and motion, being forced into stillness was its own kind of prison. And in that prison, medication wasn't weakness. It was survival.

Reflection on
All In

It was a Sunday when we all went together to see him at the rehab center. The place looked decent enough, close to home, the kind of facility designed to reassure families that their loved ones were being cared for. But nothing could have prepared me for the sight of him after the surgery.

He was wearing basketball shorts and a t-shirt when we arrived, but my mother had already helped him change into a light button-down — the kind men wear boating, easy and casual, something to help him look like himself. She wanted him to keep some dignity. He sat in the chair, one leg wrapped, rolling himself back and forth in short, restless motions. It wasn't freedom. It was confinement — a man who once ran at full force now reduced to a square of tile and the slow creak of wheels.

His eyes said more than his posture ever could. Distant. Hollow. Like a lion who had finally realized the wild it once roared through was gone — foreign, unreachable, belonging now to memory instead of instinct.

Around us, the other residents watched. Some smiled, warmed by the sight of family filling the room with noise and love. Others stared off, eyes quietly marking time. Some looked grateful. Some resigned. My father was somewhere else entirely.

Out in the smoking yard, a cigar burned in the ashtray, waiting. He went back to it again and again, drawing from it as if it were oxygen. For him, each puff was defiance — a way of saying that if he couldn't control his body, he could at least control the terms of its decline. For him, life in that chair wasn't life. And every cigar was his way of pushing back against the charade.

And as he declined, so did the house. The leaks returned with every storm. Buckets stood in their usual places. Extension cords snaked across the floor to keep one room powered by another. The house was still alive, but only in patches — still hosting Shabbat dinners, still holding holiday meals, still serving as the center of gravity because my mother refused to let it die.

But I knew what I was seeing. A man kept alive by ritual, and a house kept alive the same way. Both were running on habit. Both collapsing from the inside. Both carrying dignity only because someone refused to stop showing up for them.

Reflection on
The River

I remember the first call came from my sister. I was still at work, late Friday afternoon — maybe four, five o'clock, the time I usually tried to slip out early to get home before Shabbat. She said the rehab center had called. He'd fallen. They had to call medical services. He was on his way to the hospital.

I told her I'd call her back once I got in the car. And when I did, the second call was worse. The hospital hadn't said he was gone, but the words they used weren't comforting either. Not "stable," not "recovering." Just enough to tell us we should rush, that it was bad, that we needed to gather the family. Even though, in the back of my mind, I knew what this could mean, it still didn't click. You know the worst is possible, but you don't let it land. Not until you're standing in it.

The hospital was cold. Not just the temperature, but the air itself. Too clean, too bright, too still. I remember walking in with a hundred questions tumbling through me — Is he alive? Is he gone? Did he suffer? How did it happen? No one gave us answers fast enough, and that waiting — those first minutes where time feels like it's holding its breath — were torture.

A young doctor finally met us. Calm, clinically compassionate. The kind of man who had probably delivered this same news more times than he cared to count. He explained that my father was on machines now. The machines were breathing, pumping the blood. But there wasn't much left to do. They were just keeping him there because that's what hospitals do. The way he spoke told me he'd said it before, to other families, on other nights.

When we were taken in to see him, the reality sank in. There he was, hooked up, chest rising and falling on borrowed rhythm, his body present but the man gone. My siblings stood frozen in their own grief. My mother silent beside him. For me, my mind spun through all the conversations we never had — the ones about planning, about life, about legacy, even the simple ones about nothing at all. All those moments that never happened, and now never would. That was the heaviest weight — not just losing him, but losing the chance.

And yet, in the middle of that grief, another truth surfaced. He had always said he didn't want to live as a cripple, didn't want to be tamed by a body that no longer worked. He wanted to be wild and free. And if he couldn't have that, then he wanted freedom from the cage. As unsettling as it was, as heartbreaking as it was, part of me knew this was him getting what he had asked for all along.

We each stood in silence, each of us frozen in our own emotions, boiling quietly inside. The room felt heavier than any storm, heavier than any deal gone wrong. Because this wasn't about money, or risk, or business. This was the end of a man who had lived like a lion, and who had always said he would never stay in a cage.

Reflection on
The Aftermath

At the burial site, the weight wasn't just in the air. It was in the waiting. Waiting for everyone to arrive. Waiting for the day to move forward. Waiting for this chapter to close, even though none of us wanted it to. I just wanted it behind me.

It began in the facility where his body had been kept. A shomer sat beside him, reading Tehillim, guarding him with prayer since the moment he'd been purified. We were invited to see him one last time, one by one. This wasn't a public viewing — this was family. Quiet. Private. Heavy.

When the rabbi I had requested finally arrived, things moved quickly, though not quickly enough. The prayers. The lowering. The earth. Every part of it was more than my father had ever voiced wanting for himself. He was a man who never asked for ceremony. And yet, in the end, he received more than he asked for.

Shiva was at the house. The same house that had once held so much noise now filled with prayers, guests, food, family, comfort — and the occasional nerve of a realtor who thought it appropriate to circle grief with a business card. We sat in ripped shirts, we ate, we prayed, we told stories about the man he was. Stories of his generosity. His relentlessness. His presence.

But even in that sea of people, the absence was sharp. The phone didn't ring. That silence was deafening. For years it had rung four, five times a day. His voice on the other end, always urgent, always demanding something that could usually be solved with the flick of a finger. At the time, I found it exhausting. Annoying, even. But sitting in that house without those calls, I realized what I had lost.

I knew one day I would miss the very interruptions I once resented. And here it was. The day had come. Because that's how life can be taken too: with the flick of a finger, like a kindled flame suddenly snuffed out. And all that's left is the smoke — rising, dissipating, disappearing into memory.

Even now, almost three years later, it's hard to fully submit to the fact that he is no longer available to talk to. That the phone will never ring with his voice on the other end. And so I sit with both truths: the relief of the silence, and the ache for it to break again just one more time.

Reflection on
Settling the Chips

Shiva was the first time I really experienced what it meant to sit inside that kind of structured grief. The only other time I had seen it was when my grandfather passed away back in the Cherry Hill house. I realized then how much my father and I shared the same trait: we carried things lightly on the outside — joked, stayed lighthearted — but inside, we harbored the weight. We never showed the abyss.

And that's why shiva matters. Those seven days are not just ritual — they're mercy. They keep you from being swallowed by silence, from being left alone with the darkness in your own mind. People come, they talk, they feed you, they remind you of the good, they force your days to move forward. By the time night falls, you collapse into sleep, not despair. I was grateful for everyone who came through — for the conversations, the prayers, the food, the presence.

But in my head, one thought repeated like a drumbeat: the phone isn't going to ring anymore. No more buzzing, no more voice on the other end demanding something that could be fixed with the flick of a finger. It used to drive me crazy. But now? I knew I'd miss it forever.

When shiva ended, silence came. That's when probate and legal matters began. I made the calls — to contacts I knew, to people who knew better than me — until everything funneled down to the professionals who could take the case. Signing contracts. Making sure they were the right ones.

Moving quickly, because time was not on our side. That became my mission: salvage whatever could be salvaged, give my mother as much dignity and peace as possible, and move fast because the clock was already against us.

My mother's energy was depleted. She had carried him through the end, and now she was hollowed out. Sad. Tired. Confused. Quietly hurt. Hurt that after a lifetime with him, she was left with no structure, no cushion, no security — nothing set aside for her. She didn't voice it much in those first days, but she confided in me. And I knew that pain ran deep.

The house itself mirrored him. By then, it was in foreclosure. The roof leaked with every storm. Buckets stood in their usual places. Extension cords ran across rooms to keep one area alive by feeding off another. For years it had been patchwork, never repair. Just enough to keep the roof over our heads, never enough to make it whole.

Only later did I see the symmetry. The house was him. It was deteriorating as he was deteriorating. It seemed to exist only for as long as he did, as if it had been built not to outlast him but to collapse with him. And in the end, it did.

So the empire that looked vast from the outside dissolved into probate files, creditor calls, and conversations that ended with, No, that bill will never be paid. It wasn't defiance — it was just truth. My father lived by making things move by any means necessary, and for a time it looked like an empire. But when the music stopped, the stage was bare.

And so I stepped in, not with anger, but with one mission: salvage whatever could be salvaged, give my mother a fragment of dignity and peace, and close the books before time closed them for us.

That's what it came down to in the end. Not inheritance. Not an empire. Just the responsibility to carry what was left and finish the game.

Closing Reflection: From One Story to Yours

If you've made it this far, thank you.

Not just for reading — but for staying with me through the memories, the mess, and the meaning.

Because The Final Bet isn't only about my father. It's about all of us. About the people we love, the decisions we delay, and the echoes we leave behind.

I didn't write this to cast blame. I wrote it to understand. To honor a man who lived with fire, who gave more than he had, and who left us with both blessings and burdens. My father had his flaws, but they were never rooted in malice. He fell forward, always forward. But without a foundation to catch him, every fall meant another scramble, another gamble, another survival.

And when time finally ran out, the silence was deafening. The phone no longer rang four or five times a day. No new deals, no introductions, no voice insisting it had to be handled now. That silence has been the hardest inheritance.

But silence is also a teacher. It taught me that I still have time. That my children still have time. And that the best way to honor my father isn't to repeat his chaos, but to learn from it. To carry his fire — and to build the structure he never did.

So this book isn't just his story. It's also a mirror.

I want you to see yourself in these pages, in the missed conversations, in the urgency of preparation. Because planning isn't about fear. It's about love. It's about making sure your family never has to carry silence in place of clarity.

That's why I wrote this — so my children can understand who their grandfather was. Fierce. Generous. Restless. Larger than life. And also, deeply human. A man who mastered chaos but never prepared for calm.

If his story moves you, don't let it stop at inspiration. Let it move you to act.

Pick up the phone. Have the hard conversation. Write the will. Draft the trust. Get the policy.

Because love isn't just what you say. It's what you prepare for.

And if there's one lesson that outlives him, it's this:

Life isn't easy. But it's a lot harder if you're unwilling to learn from it.

Lessons From the Table

Some lives are built on blueprints. Others on bets.

My father's life was never about recklessness — it was about belief. Belief in grit, in instinct, in momentum. He woke up every day trying to win the day. And for a long time, that was enough.

But eventually, time calls your bluff. And when it did, he left no vault, no instructions, no protection. Only echoes.

The lesson I carry is simple but not easy: love and hustle are not enough. If you want to protect what you build, you need structure. You need layers of foundation that outlive you.

Questions to Ask Yourself

- Do I have a written will or trust that spells out my wishes?

- If I couldn't speak tomorrow, would my spouse or children know where the accounts are, what the passwords are, who to call?

- Do I have life insurance that goes beyond covering a funeral — one that creates leverage for generations?

- If my income stopped tomorrow, how long could my family stand on their own?

- Do my children know the difference between wealth and income? Have I taught them how money actually moves?

Layers of Legacy to Build

1. **Legal Documents** – will, trust, power of attorney, healthcare directive.

2. **Insurance** – policies that create liquidity, opportunity, and leverage.

3. **Liquidity** – emergency funds, brokerage accounts, or cash-value vehicles to prevent forced sales.

4. **Education** – teaching your children how compounding and stewardship work.

5. **Philosophy** – values about money: how to earn it, respect it, and grow it responsibly.

6. **Community** – advisors, mentors, peers who hold you accountable to long-term thinking.

For Further Study

- *Rich Dad Poor Dad* — Robert Kiyosaki

- *Think and Grow Rich* — Napoleon Hill

- *The Jewish Phenomenon* — Steven Silbiger

- *What Would the Rockefellers Do?* — Garrett Gunderson

- *The Millionaire Next Door* — Thomas J. Stanley

Read them not just for inspiration, but for application. Pair their lessons with the questions above, and you'll begin to build the structure my father never did.

Closing Note

If my father taught me anything, it's that motion alone can take you far — but not forever. To play only for today is to gamble tomorrow away.

So learn. Act. Build. Protect. Teach your children. Write it down. Fund it. Share it.

Because in the end, the greatest bet you'll ever place is not at the table. It's at the foundation of your family.

And the only way to win… is to prepare.

Turning Lessons into Legacy

This story isn't meant to stay on these pages. It's meant to move into your life. The best way to honor what you've just read is to act — for yourself, for your family, for the generations who will carry your name.

These exercises blend reflection with action. Read them, think about them — and then write your answers down. Because if it isn't written, it isn't real.

1. The Inventory Exercise — What's on the Table?

Take stock of what you already have.

- Home(s): _______________________________
- Bank accounts: _______________________________
- Retirement accounts: _______________________________
- Insurance policies: _______________________________
- Other assets: _______________________________

Ask yourself: If I was gone tomorrow, would my family know where this is and how to access it?

☐ Yes ☐ No

Circle the ones that need clarity — that's your starting point.

2. The Silent Test — Who Would Speak for You?

Imagine you couldn't speak tomorrow. Who would step in?

- Medical decisions: _______________________________
- Financial decisions: _______________________________

Do they have legal authority (power of attorney, healthcare directive)?

☐ Yes ☐ No

If the answer is "no" or "probably," it means silence would rule.

3. The Generational Letter

Don't just pass down assets. Pass down values. Write a short letter to your children (or future children):

- What money meant to you growing up:

  ____

- What you want them to know about wealth:

  ____

- The values you hope they carry forward:

  ____

It doesn't have to be perfect. But it has to be written.

4. The Protection Layer

Look at your foundation:

☐ I have life insurance. Amount: _______________

☐ It covers: Funeral only / Family security

☐ I have a will. YES / NO

☐ I have a trust. YES / NO

Gaps to address: _______________________________

Remember: protection isn't about fear — it's about love.

5. The Rockefeller Question

Inspired by What Would the Rockefellers Do?

If you created a family trust today, what would you want it to accomplish 50 years from now?

- My trust would: _______________________________
- The values I want preserved: _______________________

Write it as if your great-grandchildren will read it.

6. The Wealth Education Plan

Knowledge is leverage — but only if applied.

Choose 2 books from this list and commit to reading them with a notebook:

- Rich Dad Poor Dad (Robert Kiyosaki)
- Think and Grow Rich (Napoleon Hill)
- The Jewish Phenomenon (Steven Silbiger)
- The Millionaire Next Door (Thomas Stanley)
- What Would the Rockefellers Do? (Garrett Gunderson)

For each book, write down 3 lessons you can apply today:

Book 1: _____________________

1.
2.
3.

Book 2: ____________________

    1.
    2.
    3.

7. The "If Not Now, When?" Audit

List three actions you've been putting off — and give them deadlines:

    1. ____________________ Date: ________
    2. ____________________ Date: ________
    3. ____________________ Date: ________

Tell someone you trust. Accountability is the bridge between intention and execution.

Closing Exercise: Your Final Bet

Finish this sentence:

The final bet I refuse to gamble with is____________________

Say it aloud. Write it down. Build your life around it.

Glossary

This glossary exists to do more than explain words. It is here to teach — to give language to the world of risk, faith, business, and legacy. Some of these words come from the casino, some from Jewish tradition, some from medicine, finance, or history. Together, they form the vocabulary of The Final Bet.

Gambling & Casino Terms

All-In

In poker, going "all-in" means pushing every last chip into the pot. There's no hedging, no holding back. My father often lived this way — in business, in deals, even in relationships. To go all-in is to risk everything on one hand, one decision.

Ante

The cost of entry. In poker, the ante is the forced bet placed at the beginning of a hand just to sit at the table. For our family, the ante was the price of starting over in America: the first house in Northeast Philly, the cab rides, the garage rented on a prayer. The ante doesn't win the game — it only lets you play.

Bluff

Pretending you have a stronger hand than you do, in order to intimidate others into folding. A bluff can win a round, but it can't win a life. My father was a master at carrying confidence even when his stack was low. Bluffing taught me how appearances can buy you time — but never permanence.

Cold Deck

A rigged or stacked deck, designed so you cannot win. It's poker slang, but also a metaphor for life circumstances where the odds are loaded against you no matter how well you play.

Dead Man's Hand

According to gambling lore, Wild Bill Hickok was holding a pair of aces and eights when he was shot dead in 1876. The "dead man's hand" came to symbolize fate, finality, and the end of a gamble. For me, it mirrors my father's last years — still playing, still betting, but against a fate that no hand could beat.

Drawing Dead

In poker, a hand that cannot possibly win, no matter what cards come next. Symbolic of moments when the outcome is already decided, even if you don't realize it yet.

The Felt

The green cloth covering a poker table, used to represent the game itself. For us, "the felt" wasn't always a casino table — it was life's arena, where every day brought a hand to be played.

The River

The final card dealt in poker. It can make or break a hand, the last chance for a miracle or disaster. In this book, "The River" symbolizes not just cards, but the finality of life — the last chapter, where everything is revealed.

Short Stack

In poker, being left with only a small pile of chips. Vulnerable, forced to play cautiously, always one hand away from elimination. My father lived much of his life like he was short-stacked, even when he projected abundance.

Still in the Game

A phrase my father used often, usually after long days or setbacks. It meant survival, resilience, defiance. It was his way of saying: I may be down, but I'm not finished.

The Last Bluff

A bluff is only powerful if others still believe in it. Toward the end, my father's rituals — the office, the lottery tickets, the chocolate at the bodega — were his last bluff. Not because they fooled anyone, but because they kept himself convinced, he was still in motion.

Jewish Traditions & Faith

Aliyah
The immigration of Jews to Israel, especially during the mass waves of the 1950s when families fled persecution in North Africa and the Middle East. My father's family was part of this aliyah, arriving with little more than stubborn pride.

Bar Mitzvah
A Jewish rite of passage for boys at age 13 (Bat Mitzvah for girls at 12), marking the assumption of religious and communal responsibilities. My Bar Mitzvah was more than a ritual — it was my father's declaration that we had "made it" in America.

Chevra Kadisha
The Jewish "holy society" that prepares a body for burial with ritual washing, prayers, and dressing in simple white garments. They performed this sacred work for my father. It reminded me that even in silence, tradition provides dignity.

Keriah
The ritual tearing of clothing during mourning, symbo-lizing the tear in the mourner's heart. At my father's burial, keriah made grief visible, reminding us it should not be hidden.

Kabbalah
A branch of Jewish mysticism that seeks hidden meaning in scripture and the universe. To scholars, it is study. To my father, it was leverage — a way he hoped the universe itself might bend in his favor.

Kiddush
The blessing recited over wine (or grape juice) to sanctify Shabbat or a Jewish holiday before the meal. It "sets apart" sacred time from ordinary time and is often led by the head of household, with cups shared around the table.

Shabbat
The Jewish Sabbath, observed from Friday evening to Saturday evening. For my father, Shabbat was sacred — non-negotiable. No matter how broke we were, the table was set, the candles lit, the wine

poured. It was ritual in the middle of chaos.

Shomer

A "guardian" who stays with the body from death until burial, reciting psalms and ensuring the deceased is never left alone. Tradition teaches that the soul hovers nearby until burial, aware of the presence of the shomer.

Tahara

The purification ritual performed by the chevra kadisha before burial. The body is washed, prayers are said, and the deceased is dressed in simple shrouds. It symbolizes equality in death and a return to purity.

Tallit

A prayer shawl worn during Jewish prayer. At burial, one corner is cut, symbolizing that the person's earthly duties are complete.

Tefillin

Small leather boxes containing verses of Torah, bound to the arm and forehead during weekday morning prayers. Though my father wasn't observant in that way, tefillin remain central symbols of Jewish faith and practice.

Tehillim

Hebrew for Psalms. Recited for comfort, healing, and merit. In burial customs, Tehillim are read continuously by a shomer (watcher) who stays with the body from death until burial.

Financial & Legal

Advance Healthcare Directive

Written instructions for medical care if you cannot decide for yourself. Typically includes a Living Will (what treatments you do/do not want) and a Healthcare Surrogate/Proxy (who makes decisions). May include or reference a DNR. Requirements vary by state.

Bridge Loan

A short-term loan used to "bridge" the gap until long-term financing is secured. Risky and expensive. My father took one to keep Vista Del Cielo alive — and it buried him deeper when the market collapsed.

Cash Flow

The money moving in and out of a household or business. My father's cash flow often looked strong but was fragile, masking more debt than surplus.

Escrow

Funds held by a neutral third party during a transaction until conditions are met. In real estate, escrow is meant to protect. For my father, it often became the waiting room for other people's exits.

Equity

The value of ownership in an asset after debts are deducted. Equity is what remains when leverage is stripped away. For us, it rarely lasted long.

Foreclosure

The legal process where a lender takes back property due to unpaid mortgage debt. Our family's home ended this way — a mirror of my father's decline.

Homestead (FL)

Florida's constitutional protection for a primary residence: significant creditor protection, property-tax exemptions, and special transfer rules at death (especially where a surviving spouse/minor children exist). Details are technical—consult Florida counsel for planning.

Legacy Planning

The act of preparing structures — wills, trusts, insurance — to ensure wealth and values are preserved across generations. The absence of legacy planning was the loudest silence my father left behind.

Line of Credit

A flexible loan allowing borrowing up to a certain limit. Useful for liquidity, dangerous when used as lifeblood. My father relied on them often.

Liquidity

How easily an asset can be converted into cash without losing value. Liquidity is what buys time. Without it, families are forced into fire sales and desperation.

Power of Attorney (POA)

A legal document granting an "agent" authority to act on your behalf (e.g., banking, real estate, business). A Durable POA remains effective if you become incapacitated. POA authority ends at death or upon revocation.

Probate

The court process that settles an estate after death: validating a will (if any), appointing a personal representative, inventorying assets, paying debts/taxes, and distributing what remains to heirs/beneficiaries.

Seller Financing

When a seller provides financing directly to a buyer instead of a bank. My father leaned on this strategy when traditional lenders wouldn't play.

Term Policy

A life insurance policy that covers a person for a set number of years, paying a benefit if death occurs within that time. It's often the most affordable entry into protection. When I woke up to the need for planning, a term policy was the first step I took.

Trust

A legal arrangement that holds assets on behalf of beneficiaries. The wealthy use them to ensure continuity. My father never created one. His trust was in himself — and when he was gone, so was the structure.

Underwriting

The process lenders use to evaluate risk before approving a loan. For my father, underwriting was always an obstacle, something to maneuver around with charm. But when the markets changed, underwriting hardened — and charm no longer worked.

Will

A legal document that states your wishes after death — who inherits, who decides, how responsibilities are passed on. My father never left one. That silence left us with probate, creditors, and questions no one could answer.

Historical & Cultural

Atlantic City Boardwalk

A stretch of casinos, arcades, rides, and neon lights along the Jersey shore. For my father, it was both play-ground and battleground — a place where he felt alive, in risk and reward.

Joe Frazier

The heavyweight champion boxer who defeated Muhammad Ali in the 1971 "Fight of the Century" and went toe-to-toe with him again in the "Thrilla in Manila." For us, he wasn't just history — he was our neighbor in Philadelphia.

September 11, 2001

The terrorist attacks that destroyed the World Trade Center in New York, killing thousands and shaking the world economy. For my father, it was also a turning point. Deals froze, liquidity vanished, and the wave he was riding began to break.

Susita

An Israeli-made car from the 1960s–70s, known for its fiberglass body and unreliability. My father nicknamed his Dafuni — "Push Me" — because it so often needed a push start. That car became a metaphor for the scrappy beginnings of his journey.

Vista Del Cielo

Spanish for "View of Heaven." The name my father gave to his last, unfinished real estate project in Miami. It was meant to touch the skyline. Instead, it collapsed with him.

Bibliography & Further Reading

The books below shaped the way I now think about wealth, legacy, and life itself. Some I discovered late, when I was already living the consequences of not knowing them sooner. Others gave language to truths I had felt but couldn't articulate. They are not just books — they are teachers.

Core Works Referenced

Gunderson, Garrett B. *What Would the Rockefellers Do?*
Barden Books, 2016.

A practical guide on how dynasties preserve wealth across
generations using trusts, insurance, and clear family structures. It
showed me that legacy isn't just about what you earn — it's
about what you protect and pass down.

Hill, Napoleon. *Think and Grow Rich.* The Ralston Society,
1937.

One of the original personal development classics. More than a
book about money, it is about mindset, imagination, and
persistence. Reading it decades after my father's rise and fall, I
saw how belief and vision can carry you far — but also how
dangerous they become without structure.

Kiyosaki, Robert T. *Rich Dad Poor Dad.* Warner Books, 1997.

The book that first made the distinction clear between assets and
liabilities. It helped me see how my father confused motion with
wealth, and how I had inherited that same confusion.

Silbiger, Steven. *The Jewish Phenomenon.* Longstreet Press,
2000.

A study of cultural and financial habits that have allowed Jewish
families to thrive across generations. For me, it was a mirror —
connecting faith, discipline, and education with financial
resilience.

Stanley, Thomas J., and William D. Danko. *The Millionaire
Next Door.* Longstreet Press, 1996.

Not about flash, but about discipline. It showed me that the real
wealthy are often invisible — frugal, intentional, prepared. The
opposite of how my father lived, and the lesson I needed most.

Additional Influences

Collins, Morgan Housel. *The Psychology of Money.* Harriman House, 2020.

A modern classic about how behavior matters more than knowledge when it comes to wealth. It helped me connect my father's compulsions with the broader truth: we don't lose money because of numbers — we lose it because of how we think.

Covey, Stephen R. *The 7 Habits of Highly Effective People.* Free Press, 1989.

A timeless guide on values, productivity, and personal leadership. Its emphasis on beginning "with the end in mind" echoes what this book is all about — planning now for the legacy you want to leave.

Dostoevsky, Fyodor. *The Gambler.* 1867.

A novel about compulsion, risk, and the illusion of control. Though written in another century, it mirrors my father's world exactly — gambling not out of greed, but out of defiance against powerlessness.

Taleb, Nassim Nicholas. *Fooled by Randomness.* Random House, 2001.

A book on chance, risk, and the role of luck in life and markets. It reminded me how much of my father's confidence was built on the illusion that he controlled outcomes — when in truth, the dice were always loaded with randomness.

Why These Books Matter

Each of these works added a piece of language, philosophy, or strategy to what became The Final Bet. They are the fence posts around the vineyard, the playbook my father never wrote down, the wisdom I had to gather piece by piece.

I recommend them not to inspire you in the abstract, but to equip you. Read them with a pen in hand. Take notes. Ask yourself how each lesson applies to your life, your family, your foundation.

Because the greatest inheritance is not money. It is knowledge, structure, and the discipline to pass both forward.

About the Author

Amos Hadad is a financial professional, storyteller, and proud son of a lion-hearted man whose life inspired *The Final Bet*. Born into a family shaped by grit, migration, and hustle, Amos grew up watching his father build empires out of instinct — and lose them the same way. Those lessons, both inspiring and devastating, forged his mission: to help others create the foundations his father never did.

Today, Amos dedicates his work to guiding families, business owners, and dreamers to transform motion into meaning, chaos into structure, and love into lasting legacy. His writing blends raw memoir with practical wealth education, drawing from both lived experience and works such as *Rich Dad Poor Dad, Think and Grow Rich, and What Would the Rockefellers Do?*

He lives in South Florida with his wife and children, where he continues to write, mentor, and work with families to build structures that protect not just assets — but futures.